D

d

D was once a little Doll,
  Dolly,
  Molly,
  Polly,
  Nolly,
  Nursy Dolly
  Little Doll !

E

e

E was once a [Eel],
  [E]
  [W]
  [I]
  [Twi]
  Tw[ly]
  Little Eel.

F

f

[F was once a little] Fish,
  [Fishy]
  [Wishy]
  [Dishy]
  [Ishy]
  [Dishy]
  [Little] Fish !

J

j

J was once a Jar of Jam,
  Jammy
  Mammy
  Clammy
  Jammy
  Sweety—Swammy
  Jar of Jam !

K

k

K was once a little Kite,
  Kity
  Whity
  Flighty
  Kity
  Out of Sighty—
  Little Kite !

L

l

L was once a little Lark,
  Larky !
  Marky !
  Harky !
  Larky !
  In the Parky,
  Little Lark !

M

m

M was once a little Mouse,
  Mousey
  Bousey
  Sousy
  Mousy
  In the Housy
  Little Mouse !

MR. NONSENSE

A Life of Edward Lear

Also by Emery Kelen

Dag Hammarskjold: A Biography
Fifty Voices of the Twentieth Century
Hammarskjold: The Dangerous Man
Hammarskjold: The Political Man
Let's Learn About the United Nations
Peace in Their Time
Peace Is an Adventure
Proverbs of Many Nations
Stamps Tell the Story of John F. Kennedy
Stamps Tell the Story of Space Travel
Stamps Tell the Story of the UN
Stamps Tell the Story of the Vatican
The Valley of Trust

Edited and annotated by Emery Kelen
Fantastic Tales, Strange Animals, Riddles, Jests, and
Prophecies of Leonardo da Vinci

MR. NONSENSE
A Life of Edward Lear

by Emery Kelen

with illustrations by   Edward Lear

Thomas Nelson Incorporated
Nashville/Camden/New York

First edition
Library of Congress Cataloging in Publication Data

Kelen, Emery.
    Mr. Nonsense: a life of Edward Lear.

    SUMMARY: Biography   of   a   nineteenth-century
Englishman known for his nonsense verse and limericks.
    Bibliography: p.
    1.   Lear, Edward, 1812–1888—Juvenile literature.
[1.   Lear, Edward, 1812–1888.   2.   Poets, English]
I.   Title.
PR4879.L2Z67   760'.092'4   [B]   [92]   73-2672
ISBN 0–8407–6278–X

Contents

MR. NONSENSE

A Life of Edward Lear

I
The Ugly Child

There was once a sad man who went to see a doctor to be cured of his melancholy. The doctor examined him thoroughly and said, "I can't find anything wrong with you, but I have some advice. There is a circus in town; go there tonight. You'll see a clown who is so funny that you won't stop laughing for a week."

"Doctor," said the sad patient. "I am the clown."

Sometimes a joke reflects a deep human truth. The story I have just told comes to my mind when I think of Edward Lear, who, according to the opinion of his friends, was one of the funniest and most delightful men one can imagine. His great charm and humor were reflected in his nonsense books, which were greatly enjoyed by the people of his time, young and old alike. Even though some of his humor seems old-fashioned to us today, there is yet to be a generation of children that is not entertained by the man who called himself Derry down Derry, who loved to see little folks merry.

9

Lear was a great literary clown, but all the same, he was a sad man. From the very first, his life struck a sorrowful note. He was born in 1812, the twentieth in a succession of twenty-one children, and by the time he arrived upon the scene his mother had no love left for him at all. She refused to have anything to do with him.

Edward was ugly, pale, and sickly, an altogether unpromising baby who looked as if he might soon give up the ghost. Several of his brothers and sisters had died soon after birth, and since the Lear parents insisted on bestowing the same name on their babies until one stuck, there had already been three Sarahs, three Henrys, and two Catherines in a row. Out of the crowd, fifteen children survived their childhood.

Edward's father, Jeremiah Lear, was a stockbroker in London, and for some years, while the older children were growing up, he provided for his family quite well. He bought for them a great rambling house at Holloway, where he owned no fewer than twelve carriages to take them all on their Sunday outings.

Unhappily, Jeremiah Lear could not really afford such luxuries, and he fell deeper and deeper into debt. Edward was just four years old when grave financial troubles overtook his father. There is even a story that he was declared bankrupt and was shut up in debtors' prison. The twelve carriages were sold, the great house rented, the servants dismissed, and the family cast out of their suburban paradise.

> *In dreary silence down the bustling road*
> *The Lears with all their goods and chattels rode....*

Thus wrote Edward, much later, in describing those evil days. His elder sisters, he said, were put out to work as governesses, and within four months four of them had died of hardship. The younger members went with their mother to live in "horrid New Street," where Mrs. Lear used up her remaining resources in preparing a full six-course meal for their father every day, which she took to him in the prison in a basket.

It is not known how much of this heartrending tale is true and how much of it Lear made up. After all, he was a caricaturist, and he found it natural to make a grotesque joke out of hard luck. It is certain, however, that the Lears did fall on hard times, that the family lost their home and financial security, and that the grown children went out to work.

Little Edward, ugly and unloved, and probably painfully aware of his mother's dislike for him, went to be looked after by his eldest sister, Ann, a young woman of twenty-six, who was spared the dismal fate of her sisters by having a tiny income of her own, left her by her grandmother. Ann seems to have been a charming person, the sort of lady Dickens might have invented, combining churchgoing convictions with a kind and loving heart. A strong bond of affection was forged between her and her young brother. She devoted herself to Edward, and she never married, although she might have done so.

Ann could not afford to give her brother the usual schooling of a young gentleman, but she had been quite well educated herself, and she became his tutor and his school. More important, she was a clever artist and gave Edward his first drawing lessons, since it was obvious from the beginning that this was his main gift. Under her instruction, he learned to observe and to draw in minute detail flowers, butterflies, birds—all the objects of nature. He was fond of reading too, and grew up under the influence of Byron, Shelley, and Keats, the romantic poets who were at the height of their popularity at the time.

At fourteen he began to write verse himself, some of it quite serious. However, from Lear's pen, the words, even when they started out lyrically enough, tended to take a queer and eccentric twist. In his early teens, being quite taken with the charms of a little girl, he wrote in best romantic fashion of her "lovely face so pale and wan," but then he continued:

> Your high cheek-bones:—your screwed up mouth,
> How beautiful they be!
> And your eyes that ogle from north to south
> With a high diddle-diddledy-dee.

On Ann's birthday he wrote a poem of a hundred lines, every one rhyming with a word ending in "-ation." It must have been one of the most tiresome poems in the English language.

By the time Edward was fifteen, his father, now in his seventies, was safely out of jail and retired on what remained of his fortune. Edward had not a penny to his name except what Ann gave him, so he began to draw, as he put it, "for bread and butter." He did "uncommon queer shop-sketches—selling them for prices varying from ninepence to four shillings: coloring prints, screens and fans." He also made money by drawing in morbid detail pictures of diseased organs for the use of hospitals and doctors.

There was every reason for Edward Lear to be interested in the details of illnesses. Asthma, perpetual colds, and a generally shaky constitution had plagued him from babyhood. When he was six he had an epileptic attack, and he suffered from epilepsy all his life. As a youth he often had as many as two or three attacks a day.

At eighteen Lear began to give drawing lessons. Then, one day, there came a real stroke of fortune: he was engaged by the Royal Zoological Society to make drawings of the parrots in the Regent's Park Zoo.

Parrots were considered exciting birds in those days. England was expanding her empire to exotic tropical lands, and explorers brought back parrots and other hardy birds as souvenirs of their far-flung adventures, like living jewels. The Regent's Park Zoo, still one of the great zoos of the world today, had a notable collection of parrots, which was the wonder and delight of visitors.

Lear set to painting parrots, and he developed quite a passion for them. As every artist knows, when you study something intently and try to re-create it in an artistic medium, you almost have to become that very thing. That is exactly what happened to young Edward; he lived and breathed parrots for so long that he practically turned into one. He wrote to a friend that when he died, if his soul should be reborn into another life and form, he was sure it would be uncomfortable in any other shape but that of a parrot. Then and there he drew a portrait of himself with a parrot roosting on his head. Later on, his lively little cartoon parrots became engaging decorations in his books.

The naturalistic paintings of parrots that Lear produced for the Zoological Society are less familiar than his comic parrots, but they are really excellent examples of zoological paintings, both in their animated quality and their accurate detail. His portfolio of forty-two colored lithographs was very well received, and some people compared his paintings favorably to the beautiful works of Audubon. It was quite a triumph for a nineteen-year-old boy, and he began to receive commissions to illustrate the books of famous naturalists.

For the next few years Lear was up to his ears in ter-

rapins and turtles, Indian pheasants and toucans. Nevertheless, it is interesting to see that even the most naturalistic of his zoological studies are endowed with a little
touch of humor and a sense of animal intelligence. His
parrots and owls often have a purposeful or even
mischievous expression; his monkeys look even more like
little people than monkeys have a right to do. Since he
always drew from life—unlike some zoological artists who
drew from dead animals and birds—life shines in his work.

In spite of his success, however, Lear did not lay the
foundation for fame or fortune. He was paid very little for
his work, and money struggles obliged him to sell some of
his best pictures to the well-known zoological artist John
Gould, who then coolly took the credit. Gould is remembered especially as the illustrator of Darwin's *Voyage
of the Beagle,* but there is no doubt that some of the
drawings made for that famous book were actually the
work of Edward Lear. After Gould's death, Lear, who was
not given to boastfulness, wrote, "In this earliest phase of
his bird-drawing, he owed everything to his excellent wife
and myself."

Hard work with little reward was to be the lifelong fate
of the man who became known as Mr. Nonsense. But in
those days of hopeful youth, he once told a friend that he
would rather be at the bottom of the River Thames than
be in debt for one week.

II

Knowsley

The caricature that Lear drew of himself when he was nineteen years old shows a tall young man in goggles. To this self-portrait, he added the cheerful comment: "Both my knees are fractured from being run over which has made them peculiarly crooked ... my neck is singularly long ... a most elephantine nose ... and a disposition to tumble here and there owing to being half-blind."

Then one day in 1832, while this unprepossessing person was painting in Regent's Park, fate, in the person of Lord Stanley, the president of the Zoological Society, came and stood behind him. Stanley was a subscriber—one of those who put up the money—to Lear's parrot album; moreover, he was the son and heir of the twelfth Earl of Derby, and since animals were his hobby, he had collected a famous private menagerie at the family seat at Knowsley, near Liverpool.

On this fateful day Lord Stanley had looked up Lear to

ask if he would care to come to Knowsley and paint the animals of his zoo. Lear accepted the commission, not knowing, as none of us ever do know, that he had come to a bend in the road that would take him to a far more spectacular way of life than a humble illustrator had any right to expect.

In nineteenth-century England, there were great gaps between the different classes of people, and even between classes-within-classes. As the son of a stockbroker, Edward was a mere tradesman's son, a member of the "respectable" middle class, doomed, in the natural order of things, to remain modestly in his place as an inferior to the landowning squires and noblemen who dominated the nation. Of course, people of genius or those singularly gifted with moneymaking abilities might "rise in the world," but Edward was doubly doomed by the absence of any useful or prestigious gift—or so anyone would have assumed at the time.

From the modest lodgings that he shared with Ann in London he went to Knowsley, one of the great estates of nineteenth-century England. It was a huge, ancient, rambling mass of stone built in the thirteenth century and still ruled, in feudal grandeur, by the same family to which it had fallen by marriage when it was only a hundred years old. At the head of the household was the Earl of Derby himself, eighty years old and patriarch to an immense troop of children, grandchildren, and great-grandchildren, as well as sisters, brothers, cousins, and their descendants. In a great house like Knowsley there was a place even for distant connections, and an ordinary dinner would include several dozen people.

The twelfth earl was a particularly sociable soul, but the product of a jollier time, when the Prince Regent (later

George IV) ruled, who liked to gamble and drink his friends under the table. Lord Derby had a great reputation as once having been a gay blade, and in his old age he continued to love good company. He therefore filled Knowsley with friends and cronies from London, or, failing them, with people from the countryside round about, who would forgather weekly to feast in his huge hall. All his friends' friends, relations, and children were invited too, and the care of this multitude was in the hands of an even greater multitude of servants. Food for all of them and their horses and for the dogs, tame deer, flocks of partridges, and running game, and supplies for every sort of need were provided by the vast estate of Knowsley, which rolled for miles about with gardens, lawns, and games courts.

To this great monument to history, wealth, and power came the obscure young Lear, trembling at the knees and feeling perhaps not unlike other youths of his time when they entered an ancient university and were unsure of their ability to make the grade.

Naturally Lear did not go to Knowsley as an equal. He was received by the steward like any other employee, given a modest room, and told to take his meals in the steward's quarters. Edward took this quite for granted, even with relief. As he said himself, he had no experience at all in "mixing with company and society." Besides, he was miserably self-conscious on account of his ugliness, and he wore vile, untidy clothes, not only because he was poor, but also because he thought that such an ugly person should not care what he wore.

He started out at Knowsley, humble and unnoticed, getting up very early in the morning when the animals and birds at the zoo were at their liveliest and friendliest, and before the nobler inhabitants of the great house had started their commotion. In the evening he sat in the steward's room.

Then, by and by, the earl's young grandsons began to drop in on Lear, boys of his own age, or not much younger. He must have been gratified, although very likely he did not ask himself why they came, but only chatted with them and showed them the sketches he was making.

Lord Derby was far too fond of company not to notice the vacancies at his table. Where were the youngsters disappearing to so nimbly after their meal? he wanted to know. He was told about the young artist in the steward's room who was such good company that the boys could hardly wait for the meal to end before slipping off.

Lord Derby had an immediate solution to the problem: If Edward Lear was such good company, let him come upstairs to the big table and give them all the benefit of it.

And so, in that way, Lear left the respectable middle class behind him forever. He was an instant favorite with the Stanley family and their friends, and soon he was not only dining with them, but also having tea and cakes with them, and having his glass plied with champagne by earls.

All this attention from the great world did not turn Lear's head one bit. He wrote to a friend about the "uniform apathetic tone assumed by lofty society," and he said there was "nothing I long for half so much as to giggle heartily and hop on one leg down the great gallery—but I dare not."

He could not imagine why the picturesque old Earl of Wilton, who liked to wear a crimson suit and a black velvet waistcoat, should have taken such a fancy to him, and to solve this mystery he asked a lady why she thought so. The lady laughed and replied mischievously that probably since the earl was a very vain man he liked to bask in the admiring glances thrown at him by the artistic Mr. Lear.

The real reason would not have crossed the lady's lips, for people then were not given to paying compliments to the young, and possibly Lear never did realize completely one of the mainsprings of his genius. As if to make up for those close-set, peering eyes, that terrible nose, that skinny neck, and the inelegant weak physique, nature had also endowed Edward Lear with a double dose of charm, a joyous quality that attracted people and infected them.

Perhaps charm, like noses, takes different shapes in different people. In Lear's case one part of his attraction was undoubtedly founded on the fact that he was a man who never quite grew up. Perhaps we might hazard a guess that having been deprived as a baby of his mother's love prompted him to seek perpetually the affection of others. For him, this immense need carried the seeds of adult tragedy, because he was afflicted with oversensitivity and a fear that he was not loved enough. Those around him reaped the benefit of it, of course—the humor and bounce, the endearing need for love, the willing, unreserved response to any kindness. These unaffected qualities of childhood belonged to Lear even when he was an old man, and made people love him. Many of those who were captivated by him at Knowsley, were, to his perfect amazement, still among his best friends a half century later.

Of the many highly placed people who passed through Knowsley in Lear's young years, only two were to be known far beyond England or to be long remembered. The first was the kindly earl himself, who was the founder of the famous Derby Stakes, a horse race held near London every year. The second was Lear. Even then he was laying the foundation of his fame, not indeed, as he thought, by getting up early to paint Lord Stanley's animals, but by spending hours with all the littlest Stanleys and their friends and relations in the nursery, where no doubt it was permitted to giggle and hop about on one foot. There he would sing to the children, for he loved to sing; he would play tunes, for he was very clever at making up tunes; and they would gather around while he drew for them absurd animals and ridiculous old men.

Possibly Lear read to them from a very popular book containing limericks, entitled *Anecdotes and Adventures of Fifteen Gentlemen,* which had recently been published, and when he came to the end of the book he could always make up better and wilder limericks himself. Years later, he was to write the famous lines:

> *There was an old Derry down Derry*
> *Who loved to make little folks merry,*
> *So he wrote them a book*
> *And with laughter they shook*
> *At the fun of that Derry down Derry.*

That is where Lear's nonsense started—in the Knowsley nursery. He lived at or visited the house on and off over a period of years, and there was always a fresh crop of children. As the older ones outgrew their youth, they became friends and companions with whom he traveled and corresponded. The successive earls of Derby remained his patrons all his life.

During those years as an intimate of the great house he acquired the manners, habits, and attitudes of mind of what was then called a gentleman, and through conversation with "half the fine people of the day" and access to a fine library and galleries of art he acquired—however haphazardly—a gentleman's education.

Nevertheless, there was a part of his life that he kept secret from all but those who knew him best: his epilepsy. Fortunately his frequent bouts were preceded by a visual disturbance—*aura epileptica* is the scientific name—that forewarned him, so that, wherever he was, he was able to excuse himself and retire to bear his torment in the privacy of his room.

III

The Dirty
Landscape Painter

After he had been at work on the Knowsley animals and
on other zoological commissions for about five years, Lear,
in his early twenties, had to stand up to a grievous blow.
The career, which had begun with such promise and on
which he had hoped to found his life, would have to be
given up. His eyesight was failing him, and he could no
longer bear to do the close work and minute observation
necessary to produce, in the exact detail needed for zoological work, the subtly patterned garb of animals and
birds. He realized that if he continued, he would probably
lose his sight.

For some time, as a matter of course, Lear had been
giving drawing lessons to the young Stanleys at Knowsley,
and sometimes in the summer he took them on sketching
trips. They were really what we would now call "hikes,"
but in those days, before cameras were household items, it

was the custom for young gentlemen to range the countryside, carrying such artists' gear as sketchbooks, paints, and easels. Then they unpacked them at suitable spots and sketched the beauties of nature or other sights so that the pictures could be brought home as souvenirs, like snapshots. Sometimes, with his older pupils, Lear went far afield to England's beautiful Lake District or to Ireland, endlessly delightful to the artistic eye.

These trips were more educational for Edward than they were for his pupils. He had an eye for landscape. In fact, as his eyesight failed him at close work, he decided that he would become a landscape painter, and he began to study the work of his great contemporaries in this field, notably Turner, of whose work it was said, "Study the Almighty first, and Turner next."

His work at Knowsley done, Lear returned to London, and since his only training in art had been the lessons of his sister Ann, he decided to enter an art school. He did not stay there long. Perhaps he did not have enough money to sustain himself in school, or perhaps another stroke of ill fortune interfered with his plans, for at that time the asthma and bronchitis that had troubled him from childhood took a turn for the worse. Indeed, his health had been worsening steadily at Knowsley, which lies rather to the north of England, in the path of the damp gales that sweep in from the Irish Sea.

Lear's Stanley family friends did not fail to notice his illness. The old Earl of Derby had died, but the thirteenth earl, Lear's first benefactor, now insisted that Lear spend the winter of 1837, at his expense, in the warmer, healthier climate of Italy.

Lear's trip abroad marked a second turning point in his life, for he did not return to England for four years. He

settled in Rome as a landscape artist, working in watercol-
or and lithograph, and his paintings found a market
among English people living or traveling abroad. The pos-
sibility of making a modest living in this way, plus his ill
health, set the pattern for the rest of Lear's life. He
became an expatriate and something of a gypsy, for in
spite of his infirmities Lear had a venturesome spirit. It
took him roaming about the countries of the Mediterranean in search of little scenes of beauty or drama that
affluent Victorians at home would want to preserve in
small frames on their well-filled walls.

Lear climbed the sides of volcanoes, explored ancient
cities, made friends with strange people, learned smatter-
ings of many languages, and walked endlessly over
ground made famous by poets from Homer to Lord Byron.
Everywhere he went, he sketched; he made hundreds and
thousands of sketches and watercolors.

In 1841, Lear returned to England, mostly to see his
sister Ann, but also to publish a book of drawings he had
made of Roman scenes. When he returned to Rome, he
tried to persuade Ann to come and live with him there,
but she declined, feeling that her presence would add
complications to his life. She spent the rest of her days in
lodging houses or visited random relatives, happy only in
the knowledge that her beloved brother shared his life
with her through faithful letters.

Lear's loyalty to Ann and his loneliness for his friends
kept him busy writing letters home, recounting the many
adventures and misadventures of which he was the comic,
long-suffering hero. Thus from his surviving correspondence we learn a great deal about the hazards faced
by travelers in the nineteenth century. In Sicily, we are
told, he shared his bed with "vermin of two species (polite-

ly called B flats and F sharps)." In Greece he fell off his horse and was straightaway bitten by "a centipede or some horror," which caused a great swelling on his leg. Then he went out without his umbrella and got sunstroke.

In Macedonia he incensed a whole community of Moslems who caught him drawing a picture, because their religion forbids the drawing and painting of human beings. They surrounded him with cries of "*Shaitan! Shaitan!*" pelted him with stones, and seized his sketchbooks, pointing to the sky, where Allah was presumably looking down irately upon his behavior.

One night in Greece, after he had scrambled for fifteen hours on horseback over a rough mountain path, he dismounted in utter blackness while his guide went off to find weathertight shelter. Casually he sat down on what he supposed to be a bank, but a grunting and heaving convinced him of error as "a dark bovine quadruped" suddenly rose up under him and tilted him into the mud. Scrambling to his feet, Lear called out:

> *There was an old man who said, 'Now,*
> *I'll sit down on the horns of that cow!'* "

His wanderings took him to places of the earth where few Englishmen had gone. In Durazzo, Albania, the bey—the Turkish ruler of the district—was a boy of sixteen, whose sad eminence greatly touched Lear's heart. They could not talk together, but Lear, longing to see the boy smile, began to draw pictures. He drew a train and said, "Rattle-attle-attle-attle!" and then a steamboat, saying, "Wishwashsquishsquash!" and so on until he had the pleasure of seeing the boy roaring with laughter.

In the Holy Land there was more trouble with Arabs who nipped his ears, pinched his arms, pulled his beard, and tore open his pockets to rifle them of everything they contained "from dollars and penknives to handkerchieves and hard-boiled eggs." Such adventures were often dangerous, and in spite of their humorous retelling, we sense that Lear must have been a very courageous man.

We find, too, that he was made crotchety by noise. In Paris he suffered from "four hundred and seventy-three cats making an infernal row in the garden." At a Swiss hotel, "forty little ill-conducted beasts of children made a frightful noise." In Rome "a vile, beastly, rottenheaded, foolbegotten, pernicious, priggish, screaming, tearing, roaring, perplexing, splitmecrackel, crachimecriggle, insane ass of a woman is practicing howling below-stairs with a brute of a singing master so horribly that my head is nearly off."

Traveling in countries where the barber customarily spat on the soap before preparing the lather was what originally made Lear think it advisable to grow a beard, but he always shaved it off when he returned to England. Much later, in Cairo, Egypt, when he was forty-two, he grew the bushy beard that remained with him for the rest of his life and became his trademark.

On many of his travels Lear was accompanied by friends, sometimes members of the Stanley family. His prestigious acquaintances protected him and gained him acceptance in the rigid social groups and cliques that characterized English communities abroad. Occasionally, fearsome snobbery caught up with him. Once, staying at an inn in Calabria, Lear overheard two Englishmen conversing. "Do you know who that fellow is we were talking to last night?" said one. "Why, he's nothing but a dirty landscape painter."

Gleefully Lear accepted the title, and he often signed his letters, "Edward Lear, Dirty Landscape Painter."

IV
Toil and Trouble

Returning from his expeditions, Lear always went to work to put his sketches in shape for sale. Laziness was certainly not his besetting sin. Rising at half past four in the morning, he worked without stopping until dusk, and sometimes, even after dark he was still applying his sketches to canvas. And yet he wrote, "I wish I could paint faster and better and had twenty pairs of hands not to speak of an elephant's trunk to pick up any brushes when they fall down."

Lear was immensely prolific, and increasingly so with the years. In one year alone, in 1865, he produced 200 sketches in Crete, 125 in Nice, Antibes, and Cannes. In his old age, when he was quite ill, during six months in India he dispatched 560 drawings, large and small, to England, besides nine small sketchbooks. When he died at seventy-six, he was to leave a friend no fewer than ten thousand watercolors.

He exhibited his work for sale at his lodgings in Rome or whatever place he happened to be calling home at the time. His countrymen came to view them and bought them as keepsakes or souvenirs to be sent back to England. It was by no means a rich life. Besides, no sooner did he feel money in his pocket than he would send some to Ann or to some impecunious relative—for instance, two nephews who had gone to America to seek their fortunes did not find them, and sponged on Lear. If by chance nobody was asking him for money, Lear could always send something to Ann's favorite blind man, who stood at the corner of her street. Thrift was not one of his cardinal virtues, but charitableness was.

Severe financial problems always lurked around the corner, and when he came face to face with them, it took great spurts of industry to stave off disaster. Often the kindness of well-to-do friends rescued him for a while, until his modest debts, piling up, became mountainous around his ears once more. During one of his periods of hard luck, Lear tried advertising his pictures for "wedding or birthday presents . . . of most sizes and prizes."

Most of the paintings that were not bought by tourists were bought by friends, especially those who owned great attics in which to store them, or else they gave them away to some obscure gallery. The tragedy is that the more landscapes Lear produced, the more there were on the market or given away, and the more valueless they seemed.

In all his long life, his paintings were never really appreciated at their true worth. The London critics whose praise could have made him successful, and who certainly praised far worse efforts than his, never saw his work properly because at that time people were looking for something else in art than what Lear was doing.

Every artist is judged according to the values of his time, sometimes unjustly. In Lear's time, artistic tastes were moving away from strict naturalism toward poetic suggestiveness. The trend would soon find expression in the "impressionistic school." In the mid-nineteenth century the Pre-Raphaelite Brotherhood, under the leadership of Dante Gabriel Rossetti, was the precursor of this mood. Lear's paintings were therefore criticized in London for being too literal in their detail. In other words, the very quality that had made his zoological drawings so fine was held against his landscapes, which were blamed for being overaccurate and fussy in detail, with every rock or landfall so described that, as one viewer said, one could tell the geology of a countryside by looking at a painting of Lear's.

Nor did Lear's landscapes reflect the immense personal charm that rushed forth from his brush when he painted birds and animals. Sometimes he enlivened his pictures by adding human figures, but these serious "lifelike" studies of peasants working the fields or women around a well had not half as much life in them as any one of the ridiculous old men pursued by bees or cows that were to people his caricatures.

Yet he was an artist of individuality who produced works of beauty and enduring worth. In searching for reasons why he was so unappreciated in his lifetime, critics have said that some of his paintings seem labored because that is, after all, what they were: his labor to make a living. That, however, is not a convincing explanation. Leonardo da Vinci and Michelangelo also were making a living. Lear's main fault may have been that his anxiety showed. Lack of appreciation perpetually undermined his confidence in his own abilities. Once he wrote to a friend, "I certainly do hate the act of painting, and although day after day I go steadily on, it is like grinding my nose off." And he said, "It is true I don't expect to improve, because I am aware of my peculiar incapacities for art, mental and physical."

The truth is that Lear suffered from chronic melancholy, his moods of merriment and sociability alternating with spells of deep depression. The roots of his suffering lay far deeper than dissatisfaction with his work. They are to be found in his physical and hereditary constitution, his mobile emotional makeup, so often seen in fat people, especially fat humorists, and his epilepsy and general ill health. All of these excellent reasons for misery were aggravated by a wretched childhood as an unloved son, a lack of education in his chosen profession, poverty, and a feeling of failure.

He could be swiftly awakened from his mumps and grumps by a kind and companionable friend. Then, glowing with natural wit and charm, he could give back far more than he received in companionship. But depression outweighed cheerfulness, because he was spending his life doing work that was not natural to him, and sometimes in the depths of discouragement, he destroyed many of his sketches.

Beneath the thick layer of sadness Lear was aware of a feeling of buoyancy that was being denied. Once he wrote sadly to a painter friend, "There is a vein of poetry within me that ought to have come out"—and here his pessimism took over again—"though I begin to doubt if it ever will."

"No education in art—late attention and bad eyes all are against me," he wrote. He never did learn to paint properly in oils—and it was oil paintings rather than watercolors that the Victorians prized most highly as decorations for their ornate thick walls. He painted his first two oils at the age of twenty-eight. Much later, when he was forty, he applied himself seriously to learning oil techniques under the tutelage of a painter friend, William Holman Hunt, one of the Pre-Raphaelite Brotherhood, who liked Lear sufficiently to take him under his wing.

Hunt was fifteen years younger than Lear, but Lear, with his usual endearing humility, looked up to him as an artistic master and called him "Daddy." Hunt took Lear seriously as an artist but did not greatly admire his oils. Nevertheless, success followed his efforts. When one of Lear's paintings, the huge, five-foot-long "The Quarries of Syracuse," was accepted for exhibition by the Royal Academy of Arts, Lear, as one of his friends said, "goes everywhere saying that Hunt taught him all he knows." Lear told Hunt, "I am now going out to hop on one leg all the way to Hastings."

The accusation that Lear painted nature too slavishly and that he failed to put something of his own feeling into his pictures can perhaps be dismissed as the bad mood of some hairsplitting art critic. As every artist knows, nature is nature, and it is impossible for an artist to paint it without having his own personal feelings filter through the image. Certainly some painters leave the viewer more room for imagination than others do. But if Lear chose to place in the same picture the structure of a leaf and then, far away, the meticulously molded structure of a mountain range, he did at least create a sensation of immense space between them. This was the sort of personal feeling and personal thought that Lear put into his paintings, whether the critics were open to it or not.

Mostly he worked in watercolors. His method was to dip a brush into a large wide-necked bottle of color and, after one or two touches, to carry the painting to the end of the room and waltz back to inspect it from a distance. This performance was repeated, Lear dipping, flicking at several pictures at a time, until a row of them was arranged across the room, with the artist waltzing back and forth between them. That, of course, is not the ideal way to produce good paintings. Lear's offhand methods certainly appalled William Holman Hunt. It was the necessity of producing a great many paintings to be sold in quantity at low prices that prompted Lear to invent these assembly-line tactics.

Lear's watercolors have been called—again perhaps unjustly—mere colored drawings. But this criticism rests on narrow technical grounds. It really does not matter whether an artist chooses to paint with a brush, with a spatula, or with his fingernails, or what specific routine he uses to achieve his effects. Leonardo da Vinci was continually experimenting with one technique or another. An artist works and touches and peers and smears and repairs until at last the waltz is over and he has done the best he can for the moment.

The works of the "dirty landscape painter" Edward Lear are, to be sure, not equal in quality, but some of them are very good. As he grew older, his strict adherence to precise naturalism loosened, perhaps because by then his eyesight had become a serious hindrance. In any case, judging by today's tastes, his later paintings are his best.

V

The Derry
Down Derry

In 1845 Lear was in England again, working hard on sketches for a travel book about his journeys in Italy the two previous summers. The book was to be expensively produced and sold by subscription to his rich friends. In addition, he spent almost all his spare time—and to this day no one has discovered why he took it into his head to do so—preparing for publication *A Book of Nonsense*, a collection of verse, limericks mostly, that he had composed years before to amuse Lord Derby's youngsters in the Knowsley nursery. It is quite possible that those same children, now grown and filling nurseries of their own, themselves persuaded Lear to publish the remembered rhymes.

Lear, worried that such absurdities, if publicly acknowledged, might damage his reputation as a sober-minded landscape painter, did not sign his real name to the first edition, but gave himself a pen name, Derry down Derry, and even a pleasing new appearance, drawing the author as a plump little man with a turned-up nose.

The title page of Lear's first Book of Nonsense. The happy gentleman is probably Lear's publisher.

A *Book of Nonsense*, published in 1846, was an immediate success. Within very short order not only children but their parents, too, all over England, were reading it with delight. Even then, Lear, who was far from a financial wizard, did not guess that such a book might reap him riches beyond his wildest dreams. After the third reprint, he offered to sell his publishers the copyright of the book outright for one hundred pounds, but the publishers, who were not financial wizards either, hesitated. When a new edition of two thousand copies was sold out immediately, they changed their minds. By that time, however, Lear had also changed his; he would not take a penny less than £125. He got it. That was his only profit from a book that is still selling and that even in his lifetime went into nineteen editions.

At no time in his life did Lear suspect that, in writing and drawing nonsense, he had hit upon the work that the angels had created him to do. Still, he did learn to take pleasure and pride in the work. It delighted him once in a bookshop to see three young men, who had just bought a copy of his book, going into fits over it. Like other authors, he was very hurt when some glum critic in the *Saturday Review* gave him credit only for "persistent absurdity," and called his book (with singular injustice) "a reprint of old nursery rhymes."

Lear complained to a friend, "I wish I could have all the credit due to me, small as that may be. I wish someone would review it properly and funnily."

There had been, when the first *Book of Nonsense* appeared, considerable speculation among the public as to who the mysterious Derry down Derry actually was, and even after the second edition was published with his true name on it, people did not actually believe it. By that time Lear was thoroughly enjoying the joke, and he wrote to a young lady about an incident that, one hopes, is nothing short of truth:

I was on my way from London to Guildford, in a railway carriage, containing, besides myself, one passenger, an elderly gentleman: presently, however, two ladies entered, accompanied by two little boys. These, who had just had a copy of the "Book of Nonsense" given them, were loud in their delight, and by degrees infected the whole party with their mirth.

"How grateful," said the old gentleman to the two ladies, "all children, and parents too, ought to be to the statesman who has given his time to composing that charming book!"

(The ladies looked puzzled, as indeed was I, the author.)

"Do you not know who is the writer of it?" asked the gentleman.

"The name is 'Edward Lear,'" said one of the ladies.

"Ah!" said the first speaker, "so it is printed; but that is only a whim of the real author, the Earl of Derby. 'Edward' is his Christian name, and, as you may see, LEAR is only EARL transposed."

"But," said the lady, doubtingly, "here is a dedication to the great-grandchildren, grand-nephews, and grand-nieces of Edward, thirteenth Earl of Derby, by the author, Edward Lear."

"That," replied the other, "is simply a piece of mystification; I am in a position to know that the whole book was composed and illustrated by Lord Derby himself. In fact, there is no such a person at all as Edward Lear."

"Yet," said the other lady, "some friends of mine tell me they know Mr. Lear."

"Quite a mistake! completely a mistake!" said the old gentleman, becoming rather angry at the contradiction; "I am

Lear showing his name in his hat to prove that Edward Lear is a man and not merely a name.

well aware of what I am saying: I can inform you, no such a person as 'Edward Lear' exists!"

Hitherto I had kept silence; but as my hat was, as well as my handkerchief and stick, largely marked inside with my name, and as I happened to have in my pocket several letters addressed to me, the temptation was too great to resist; so, flashing all these articles at once on my would-be extinguisher's attention, I speedily reduced him to silence.

VI

Her Majesty's Drawing Master

The same year, 1846, that the first *Book of Nonsense* appeared under anonymous authorship, Lear proudly set his name on two other publications. One was done at the initiative of Lord Derby—that is, the former Lord Stanley and collector of the Knowsley menagerie—who decided to publish some selected drawings of Lear's under the title *Gleanings from the Menagerie at Knowsley Hall*. The other was the beautiful and expensive two-volume set, entitled *Illustrated Excursions in Italy*, which Lear had written from his travel notes. The dedication was to Lord Derby, who probably had been a major subscriber. It is rather amusing that on the last page of the second volume of this dignified work there is an advertisement for a certain anonymous *Book of Nonsense*.

On the whole, these travel books of Lear—for in the ensuing years there were to be others describing his wanderings in Italy, Greece, and the Mediterranean islands—

fulfilled a real need for stay-at-home Englishmen who looked to the classic lands as to the remote cradle of their culture.

The year 1846 was momentous for Lear for another reason also. That summer he received a summons to see Queen Victoria, then twenty-seven years old. The queen, herself an amateur artist, having seen Lear's *Illustrated Excursions* and admired his drawings, wanted him to give her a series of twelve drawing lessons.

The first few lessons were to take place at Osborne, the queen's country house on the Isle of Wight. Lear, in spite of his many friends among the aristocracy, never learned to be pompous, and when he arrived at Osborne on the appointed day, he was dressed with his customary carelessness. To the servant who answered the bell, he said simply that he had come to see the queen. The servant, puzzled, showed him into a room. There Lear was soon joined by an equerry to whom he again explained that he wished to see the queen. The equerry, convinced that he was dealing with a harmless madman, patiently and soothingly questioned him about his business with the queen until he finally unearthed the information that this was Edward Lear the artist and that he really did have an appointment to give drawing lessons to Her Majesty.

In the course of these lessons, Queen Victoria duly noted her progress in her diary.

July 15th, 1846. Osborne. Had a drawing lesson from Mr. Lear, who sketched before me and teaches remarkably well, in landscape painting in water colours.

July 16th, 1846. Osborne. Copied one of Mr. Lear's drawings and had my lesson downstairs with him. He was very pleased with my drawings and very encouraging about it.

July 17th, 1846. Osborne. I had another lesson with Mr. Lear, who much praised my 2nd copy. Later in the afternoon I went out and saw a beautiful sketch he has done of the new house.

July 18th, 1846. Osborne. After luncheon had a drawing lesson and am, I hope, improving.

The new house to which the queen referred was the present Osborne House, which was then being built under the eye of the prince consort. After the prince's death in 1861, Lear sadly recalled to a friend that the prince had once shown him a model of the new house, and particularly a terrace of which he was especially fond, and of which he said, "When we are old, we shall hope to walk up and down this terrace with our children grown up into men and women."

While Lear was quite at ease now among noblemen, he was not at all acquainted with the fine points of court etiquette, and he did not take much trouble to learn them, preferring at all times to behave himself naturally. Like many other Englishmen, he liked to spend cold days toasting himself with his back to the fireplace; probably he did not hesitate, either, to hoist his coattails up to feel the heat better. It did not occur to him that this was hardly the proper posture for a British subject to assume while standing before his queen. Each time he took up this comfortable position, a watchful gentleman-in-waiting politely invited him to see something at the far side of the room, but Lear was a long time getting the message. He repeated the blunder again and again.

The young queen, in those years when she was a wonderfully happy wife and mother, was by no means the exacting person she became in her sad widowhood. She had taken a liking to her tutor and did not hold such lapses against him. One day she showed him her personal jewels, a vast collection of diadems, crowns, bracelets, and lockets that were kept in glass display cases, where they sparkled and trembled in a riot of colored stones.

Lear exclaimed in wonder, "Oh! Where *did* you get all those beautiful things?"

Besides the fine naïveté of this question, there was another nice bungle hidden in it, for one is not supposed to address a queen as "you," but as "Your Majesty" or "Ma'am." However, the queen replied graciously, "I inherited them, Mr. Lear."

One day at Osborne Lear sketched a newly completed wing of the house, and the queen had an engraving made of it. After his return to Rome he wrote to Ann:

> One of the Queen's Ladies-in-Waiting, who is here, has delivered to me a little print engraved from one of my drawings—of Osborne House—at Her Majesty's desire. This is one trait of many that have come under my notice, that Queen Victoria has a good memory for any little condescension and kindness. I am really quite pleased with my little engraving and shall have it placed in a good frame as soon as I can get one made:—you need not, however, tell the incident to everybody: for it would look like boasting upon my part, who have done little enough to deserve so gratifying a notice.

Her Majesty's drawing master was a rather modest man.

VII

Journey
to the East

The twelve years Lear spent in Rome, with occasional trips to England, had been on the whole happy and constructive. His successes had been modest, but they had taken care of his needs, and his health had stabilized in the warmer climate.

However, the atmosphere in Italy was changing, bringing an end to the peaceful, indolent days so enjoyed by the English colony. As Lear put it, "The days of possible Lotus-eating are diminishing." The change was brought about by the restlessness of the people of Italy who, discontented and oppressed by their autocratic rulers, were commencing the struggle that would end in the revolution of 1848.

Before the menacing mood blew up, Lear, reluctant to leave a blade of grass in Italy undrawn, took another long tour with a friend to Sicily, a journey that was distinguished by an exceedingly uncomfortable climb up Mount

Etna. "We came down ridiculously fast: you stick your heels in the ashy cone and slide down almost without stopping, to the bottom."

The revolution broke out locally in the middle of a dinner party in Melito on the southernmost tip of Italy. The hostess had a violent fit and had to be carried out, "the party breaking up in the most admired disorder."

Lear returned to Rome for the winter, but spent it packing his possessions and returning them to England. The following year he spent traveling in the eastern Mediterranean, including the island of Corfu, where he was the guest of the president of the University of Corfu. According to a letter to Ann, Lear found the island to be a paradise of beauty. While there, he had the opportunity to join the party of the English diplomat, Sir Stratford Canning—"the Great Ambassador," as the Turks called him—who was on his way back to his post in Constantinople.

They stopped at Athens. "Poor old scrubby Rome sinks to nothing by the side of such beautiful magnificence," Lear wrote to Ann about the Parthenon, and set to work with his customary incredible industry to transfer most of the glory of Greece to paper. It must have given him particular pleasure that "owls, the bird of Minerva, are extremely common, and come and sit very near me when I draw."

Lear left the ambassador's party temporarily to travel on his own in Greece, of course overdoing his exertions and catching a fever, possibly malaria. He arrived in Constantinople in an exhausted state and went straight to bed, where Lady Canning had to nurse him—"as kind as 70 mothers," said Lear, who had never had even one. Gradually he recovered health and appetite and was able to write hungrily home, "No consideration of morality or sentiment or fear of punishment would prevent my devouring any small child who entered this room now. I have eaten everything in it but a wax candle and a bad lemon."

In spite of his fevers Lear had been as impressed as all visitors are by his first sight of Constantinople from the sea. "Certainly no city is so wonderfully beautiful when you first approach it," he wrote Ann, ". . . I think the perpetual change as the steamer moves on, of ruined walls, immense domes—brilliantly white minarets—and all mixed up with such magnificent cypress, pine, and plane foliage is truly wonderful."

He was much pleased by the imperturbability of Turks in the presence of foreigners, especially when witnessing the struggles of Englishmen trying to sit with dignity on the floor. "They never stare or wonder at anything: you are not bored by any questions, and I am satisfied that if you chose to take your tea while suspended by your feet from the ceiling, not a word would be said or a sign of amazement betrayed."

As the Great Ambassador's guest, he also had the rare privilege, for a foreigner, of attending the annual ceremony of foot kissing in the Seraglio, when the Sultan received all his pashas and generals from the farthest reaches of his empire and, amid silks, satins, the clangor of Eastern music, and the sweep of feathers, had his foot kissed by every one of them.

Lear had intended to extend this visit to Turkey to a really thorough tramp over the entire Near East, including the Holy Land, in the company of a friend, but they got no farther than Egypt before Lear's health, which he had not yet fully recovered, broke down again and he was obliged to interrupt the journey and return to Malta, on his way to England.

This episode is notable in Lear's life, mostly because in Malta he struck up a close friendship with Franklin Lushington, a taciturn young man, the exact opposite of the exuberant Lear. The two liked each other at once and took off to spend the spring in Greece with a short tour of the Peloponnesus, which in that season is profuse with flowers. "The whole earth is like a rich Turkey carpet," Lear wrote. "As for Lushington and I, equally fond of flowers, we gather them all day like children, and when we have stuck our hats and coats and horses all over with them—it is time to throw them away and get a new set."

Lear's friendship with Lushington was not to bring him unmarred contentment for, like most unmarried people, he would sometimes fix a too intense affection on a friend not able to return it. Some poems Lushington wrote show him to have been a person of humanity and compassion, like Lear himself, and animated by social ideals that seem very modern also in their indignation over the sufferings of the poor. However, he was also shy and inward turned and quite incapable of matching Lear's ebullient and outgoing nature, so that Lear was continually finding himself deeply offended by Lushington's aloofness. Lushington was equally exasperated by Lear's need for demonstrated affection. Yet the friendship was well founded and strong, and it continued—as was the case with most of Lear's friendships—as long as they both lived.

Another great friend and frequent companion of Lear's tramps and tours and one with whom he maintained a vivid lifelong correspondence was Chichester Fortescue— or "40scue" as Lear sometimes chose to call him—who was to make a grand career in Parliament and in Gladstone's cabinet. "I like very much what I have seen of Lear," he wrote a few days after their first meeting. "He is a good, clever, agreeable man—very friendly and *getonable* with." He commented much later that Lear was "one of those men of real feeling it is so delightful to meet in this cold-hearted world," from which one gathers that he liked in Lear those very qualities that embarrassed Lushington.

Most of Lear's friends made great careers and great names for themselves in the halls of learning or in the history books. A surprising number of them were raised to the peerage. For example, Thomas Baring, who, with his brother Evelyn Baring, was among Lear's closest friends, was created Earl of Northbrook and became viceroy of India.

This collection of grand friends is so striking that Lear has been accused of seeking out earls as companions, but no fair review of his life and ideas bears this out. To begin with, most of them were his companions long before they were created earls; moreover, he bestowed the same loving attention on all of his friends, regardless of their social position. While Lear was obviously attracted to people of quality who, in the marvelous political and economic expansion that England enjoyed during the middle years of the nineteenth century, were automatically singled out for honor and notice, they, in turn, were equally taken with him. In his own way, he too was a man of outstanding quality, one of their own kind.

Lear was sensitive, amiable, and witty. He could be moody and abrupt, even explosive, but such faults are usually forgiven an artist. On the whole, his warm regard was held out to everyone, young and old, who deserved it, and he not only loved his friends heartily but their children and their wives as well. Furthermore, he could

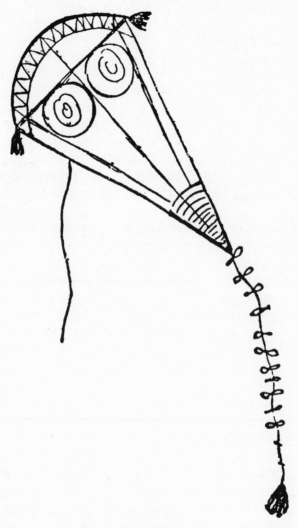

K was once a little Kite

"vamp" marvelously on the piano, making a grand trill and rattle; he could set poems to music and sing them in a soulful voice. No wonder, then, that immediately upon his arrival home in England, he was always deluged with dozens of invitations to dine and to spend long weekends in country houses.

As a young man Lear reveled in such popularity. Growing older and moodier, he became critical of the emptiness of the lives of the so-called "leisured classes" with their incessant tea and gossip, and he narrowed his visits to households where he felt most particularly at home—naturally with people of talent like himself. In the details of Lear's life one can catch a glimpse of such august persons as Alfred Lord Tennyson, Benjamin Jowett, the vice-chancellor of Oxford and translator of Plato and Thucydides, and Francis Palgrave, whose *Golden Treasury* was to become the delight and terror of English schoolchildren.

Among his favorite friends were children, not only the loved children of his friends whom he saw grow up and who remained attached to him in adulthood, but also the children of the most casual hotel acquaintances, about whom he would write with appreciation and delight to Ann and 40scue. It was for some children, met casually in a hotel, that he drew one of his favorite alphabets. Every morning, when they came to breakfast, they would find a new letter on their plates, with a poem and drawing.

He would have loved his own children if he had married. One by one, his bachelor friends, the walking and touring companions, were stolen by careers or wives from casual, everyday companionship, and more and more Lear was finding himself alone. He longed to marry, but that happiness, too, seemed beyond his reach.

VIII

The Terrible Demon

There can be no doubt that the main reason Lear was reluctant to marry was the state of his health. The attacks of epilepsy that had plagued his life from childhood abated with the years, but they remained frequent. On top of that, asthma, bronchitis, and semiblindness complicated everything he did. Unlike a more selfish type of man, Lear was too thoughtful to inflict these nuisances upon a young woman.

His epilepsy, however, may give a clue as to the sort of person he really was; almost certainly it was one of the aspects of his life that twisted him into the shape of Mr. Nonsense. We know, for example, that Lear was a tremendous traveler. The obvious reason for his restlessness is that he traveled for professional purposes, or again that he traveled for his health, perpetually fleeing excessive cold or heat or damp. Nevertheless, one glance at his timetable, year by year, shows that jumping about the Mediterranean at such a rate could not possibly have benefited a man who suffered from bronchitis, asthma, rheumatism, and a recurring fever of mysterious nature that was probably malaria.

In this short biography of Edward Lear, we cannot follow his formidable peregrinations year by year, but if we focus upon just one year, we will find it not at all unique. He might start out by traveling from Corfu to Egypt, then to the Holy Land and Lebanon and back to Corfu, and then to England, which he might very soon leave for a stay in Rome. Considering that in his day travel was hazardous, difficult, and uncomfortable and that Lear nevertheless never stopped traveling, it is more than likely that he traveled because he was driven to travel, and that it was none other than his "terrible demon," his epilepsy, that was the merciless driver.

Epilepsy is a nervous disease marked by convulsions and loss of consciousness during its worst seizures, called *grand mal* attacks. The patient falls—curiously, he always falls on the same part of his body—his muscles contract, and he loses consciousness. When he revives, after a few minutes, he does not remember anything that has happened.

Some epileptics, like Lear, are fortunate enough to have a warning when a *grand mal* attack is about to occur, such as a distortion of vision followed by a "twilight" or dreamlike state and which might last for several days. As a child, Lear had as many as three severe seizures a day, and as an adult twenty a month, so he probably went through many of these lighter phases of the disease as well. It is likely that he spent much of his life in the twilight of a dream world.

However, we are told by other talented epileptics, such as the Russian novelist Dostoevski, that this strange world is the very climate of inspiration. Perhaps it is not an accident that many extraordinarily gifted people have been epileptics.

There are several varieties of epilepsy, depending on the part of the brain that is affected, and some of them, as described in the medical textbooks, have symptoms that are characteristic of the personality of Lear. One of these symptoms is the urge to travel. Dr. Eugene Bleuler writes, "Because of their moods, they cannot remain anywhere permanently: many become tramps." It does often happen that chronic vagrants are epileptics, and it happens, too, that epileptics who live otherwise perfectly ordinary lives will sometimes, in the twilight state, buy themselves plane tickets to far-off places. Upon their arrival and recovery, they have no idea how they got there.

Nothing so extreme happened to Lear, so far as we know, but he was driven to travel, and what is more, he drove his characters, the creations of his mind, to travel also. The Owl and the Pussycat are always on the move, and so are Mr. Daddy Long Legs and Mr. Floppy Fly, who sailed toward the Gromboolian Plain, and the Jumblies forever at sea in a sieve, and the children, Violet, Slingsby, Guy, and Lionel, who went around the world. Lear ran the wildest travel bureau this side of Lake Pipple-Popple.

Another habit, typical of epileptics, that has been observed by psychologists is their tendency to collect letters and photographs and all kinds of trifles. Lear showed signs of this symptom, although it may merely have been loneliness that drove him to keep mementos as well as to travel. In his drawing room he had a long frame containing pho-

Violet,   Slingsby,   Guy, and Lionel,

who went around the world

tographs of his friends. He was continually adding to it, but here and there were blank places, showing that a friend had died. The pictures of these friends were taken from the frame in the drawing room and placed in another hanging in his bedroom. He also carefully preserved the letters he received from his friends.

The most interesting light that the medical textbooks throw on Lear's life is the clue they give to his nonsense vocabulary and his verses. Epileptics are known to like rhymes and repetition in form and content, and they often form expressions of their own invention. Lear, of course, was no ordinary man, but repeated words, rhymes, and refrains are characteristic of his poetry, as are invented words like "beeeeeeeeeeestly" or "splendidopheropherostiphongious." Although some of his expressions were wild and weird, he was a master of words. In fact, he was an inspired punster and wordsmith. He signed his letters not with kindest regards, but with "Flinkywisty Pomm Slushypipp," or some other fantastic phrase. His unheard-of animals, such as the Nupiter Piffkin, the Biscuit Buffalo, the Fimble Fowl, the Blue Boboob, the Bisky Bat, and the Cummerbund, were bred of sheer word mischief.

Alliteration was music to his ears. His writing is full of the wondrous noises that words can make: the Absolutely Abstemious Ass, the Comfortable Confidential Cow, the Enthusiastic Elephant, the Hasty Higgeldipiggledy Hen.

Lear's published work, as well as his private correspondence, is peppered with such nonsense words and games with sound. He signed a letter to a child, not "your Adopted Uncle," but "your Adopty Duncle." An elephant was in Lear's vocabulary "a Nellyphant"; there was also a certain historical character called "Mary Squeen of Cots."

Once Lear wrote a letter to a friend that reads in its entirety:

> Thrippy pilliwinx,—inkly tinsy pobblebookle abblesquabs? Flosky? Beebul trimble flosky! Okul scratchabibble-bongibo, viddle squibble tog-a-tog, ferrymoyassity amsky flamsky ramsky damsky crocklefether squiggs.
>
> Flinkywisty Pomm
> Slushypipp

Like all people who live by themselves, or are ill, Lear

was self-absorbed. His letters are minute accounts of the activities of that ever-present, ever-fascinating, altogether singular first person, I. In addition, there is a melancholy mood that runs through his writing like a somber specter stalking the pages. The reader never knows when some absurdity will suddenly dissolve into the most touching dolefulness. Although Lear never lost his gift of gaiety, and in spite of his infirmities could glitter so smartly that he lighted everyone around him with merriment, he had long periods of reasonless depression that increased as he grew older. Sometimes he would fly off the handle completely, creating violent scenes with his friends, and then humbly apologize to them afterward. A deep undercurrent of suffering shimmers through some of his most nonsensical songs, and troubles the laughing heart.

In earlier times, epileptics, with their seeming contact with a strange otherworld, were often to be found among soothsayers and priests; they exorcised demons, made oracular pronouncements, and hurled inkwells at devils. They were admired as well as feared, and epilepsy was referred to as the sacred disease.

Many geniuses have been epileptics: Dostoevski, Molière, Flaubert, Lord Byron (who was an idol of Lear), and Handel. In ancient times there were the great epileptics (all of them, incidentally, restless travelers): Alexander the Great, Julius Caesar, Mohammed and, according to some, St. Paul.

And so Lear's company in the pages of the medical textbooks is even more distinguished than that of the eminent Victorians he enjoyed knowing in life. But all of his historical companions were driven by the same cruel hand of the terrible demon.

IX
Lear
the Caricaturist

Lear, a refugee from revolution on the Continent, returned to England in May of 1849. There, for once in his life, he had the pleasure of receiving money without having to work hard for it. An old lady, a friend of the Lear family, had died and left him five hundred pounds.

Lear's satisfaction with this inheritance, however, may well have been diluted with a great deal of disappointment. For some years the old lady had been hinting that she might make him one of her chief heirs, but Lear, busy with travel and painting, and never self-seeking, had neglected her, so in the end she left the bulk of her large fortune to be divided among perpetual widows.

Lear commented to Fortescue with good humor, "I thought directly I heard of this matter that I would instantly marry one of the 30 viddies, only then it occurred to me she would not be a viddy any more if I married her."

With his small wealth in his pocket Lear now decided to try to repair what he believed to be his chief shortcoming: his deplorable lack of formal artistic training, especially the rigorous training offered at the Royal Academy School of Art. This course, which had been designed to give British artists a thorough grounding in the style of the Old Masters, took no less than ten years of intensive work, during which time it was difficult for an artist to support himself without financial resources.

Also, the requirements for the course were particularly stringent, and Lear nervously prepared "drawings from the antique" for presentation to the selectors. Great was his excitement, therefore, when in 1850 he received word that he had been accepted. "What fun—pretty little dear— he got into the Academy he did!—Yes—O so he did," he burbled in a letter to Fortescue. "I tried with 51 little boys —and 19 of us were admitted. I go with a large book and a piece of chalk to school every day like a good little boy."

The other "little boys" must have been quite surprised to find in their midst a man who was nearly thirty-eight years old, Her Majesty's drawing master, and the author of the famous Nonsense Books.

How long Lear remained at the Academy school is not known—probably no more than two and a half years, and certainly not long enough to relieve William Holman Hunt of the task of teaching him how to paint in oils. It is also open to question whether even those few years were not a sheer waste of time and effort. He could have studied at the Academy for twenty years and only strayed farther away from the art of which he was already a master— that of the caricaturist or satirist, a portrayer of human beings at their most human.

A caricaturist may learn drawing techniques at school, but the main source of his art consists in attentive and sensitive observation of human nature and, indeed, all other kinds of nature. He must learn to see, and then to express an opinion about what he sees through the use of spare and simple line.

Lear, who in the Regent's Park Zoo and at Knowsley sat all day, day after day, in front of the bird cages, learned how to see birds not only with the accurate graphic detail needed for zoological illustrations but also with an intense, deeply felt understanding. One can see this ability in his drawing, seemingly simple, of the seven young parrots who ruffled, puffled, and muffled; or in the drawing of the seven young storks who began to chitter-chatter and patter-blatter when sent away to see the world. These are surpassing caricatures, not to mention penetrating artistic creations. Perhaps Lear thought nothing much of them himself, for he was preoccupied with his ambition to hang yet another Greek ruin, in as much detail as possible and preferably in oils, on the venerable walls of the Academy. But even if his landscapes had been much better known than they were, surely none was as memorable as these lively, living bird cartoons.

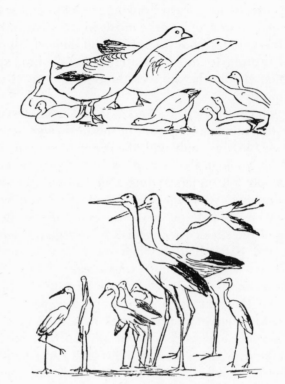

Lear must have held the belief—because he drew them that way—that men and animals bear a striking resemblance to each other, not only in looks but in characteristics. This idea is far from new. Four thousand years ago, Hammurabi, the Babylonian king and lawgiver, advised his judges that before pronouncing sentence on a defendant they would do well to evaluate his personality by his likeness to an animal. Around 300 B.C., Aristotle postulated, "There never was an animal with the form of one kind and mental characteristics of another." And he also said, "Soul and body are in sympathy."

Much later, during the sixteenth century, the Italian physicist Giambattista Della Porta, developer of the camera obscura (precursor of the photographic camera), compared the faces of men to those of animals and birds. In our own day the idea is by no means forgotten. The biologist C. R. Stockard has found some surprising similarities of behavior between certain breeds of dog and the human beings who most closely resemble them.

There can hardly be any doubt that Lear was alive to these notions, too, because he has left us many drawings of people looking comically like animals and shining in animallike situations. The theme shows up time and again in the Nonsense Books.

There was an old person of Crowle,
Who lived in the nest of an owl;
When they screamed in the nest, he screamed out with the rest,
That depressing old person of Crowle.

There was an old person of Skye,
Who waltz'd with a Bluebottle fly:
They buzz'd a sweet tune, to the light of the moon,
And entranced all the people of Skye.

There was an old person of Brill,
Who purchased a shirt with a frill;
But they said, "Don't you wish, you mayn't look like a fish,
You obsequious old person of Brill?"

There was an Old Man who said, "Hush!
I perceive a young bird in this bush!"
When they said—"Is it small?" He replied—"Not at all!
It is four times as big as the bush!"

There was an old man in a Marsh,
Whose manners were futile and harsh;
He sate on a log, and sang songs to a frog,
That instructive old man in a Marsh.

There was an old man of El Hums,
Who lived upon nothing but crumbs,
Which he picked off the ground, with the other birds round,
In the roads and the lanes of El Hums.

There was an old person of Nice,
Whose associates were usually Geese.
They walked out together, in all sorts of weather.
That affable person of Nice!

There was an old man of Dumblane,
Who greatly resembled a crane;
But they said, "Is it wrong, since your legs are so long,
To request you won't stay in Dumblane?"

For all his affinity with animals, Lear was far from being a universal animal lover. To the vast amusement of his country friends, he was extremely queasy in the presence of their horses and dogs, especially the exuberant kind of dog that likes to bound about and give a proper welcome to a guest. He was a cat lover, a different kind of person altogether from a dog lover.

In his later years, after he had settled down, Lear kept several spoiled cats. One of them, Potiphar, accompanied Lear's valet to Corfu and never came back. Lear then bought a kitten and called it Foss. Poor Foss had the misfortune to lose part of his tail at an early age, which enabled Lear to describe him as "the cat with no end of a tail."

Foss became his master's faithful companion and friend and, for that reason, something of a world celebrity both before and after his death. In Lear's last self-portraits, one can usually admire this great ugly Foss positioned somewhere near his master. In any number of the drawings, however, it is obvious that Lear never took Foss seriously as a cat, but thought of him more as a person like himself, a "lively old cove."

Foss dancing

Apart from animals, Lear's caricatures of human beings have a quality of inspired naïveté that is very appealing. They fairly bound off the page with ebullience, just as the mind of Lear continually jumped the limits of convention and common sense—"way out" we would call him today. Perhaps, artistically, these human caricatures come off second best to the birds, but they have always met with the universal approval of children, who are never averse to the sight of grown-ups laboring under some ghastly disadvantage.

Lear's human caricatures were not, however, universally admired by older people, and he gleefully recorded the remarks of a certain lady who would never "allow her grandchildren to look at my books, inasmuch as their distorted figures would injure the children's sense of the beautiful."

Lear never drew caricatures of real people in public life, "nonsense, pure and absolute, having been my aim throughout." All the same, no one in his day failed to recognize the famous hero of the limerick:

> *There was an Old Man at a Station,*
> *Who made a promiscuous oration,*
> *But they said, "Take some snuff!*
> *You have talked quite enough,*
> *You afflicting Old Man at a Station!"*

This Old Man was Prime Minister Gladstone, whom Lear did not like, and who had a habit of making speeches at railway stations to the captive audiences he found there waiting for their trains.

Another extraordinary set of Lear limericks gives us some insight into the complicated nature of Mr. Nonsense. They are the ones that concern noses.

The nose is the most significant ornament in the human face. Everyone gets just one, right in the middle, and if by any chance it is too big for popular taste, or too small, or too upturned or downturned, its owner is apt to feel that his face alone was somehow not made in God's image.

When someone is seriously at odds with the world, we say that his "nose is out of joint." When we want to disguise ourselves completely, we wear a false nose. We all feel deeply for the tragicomic hero of Rostand's play *Cyrano de Bergerac*, whose nose was too big. Though in other respects Cyrano is portrayed as an unusually gifted man, we know in our deepest heart that noses are important, and so we weep for him.

Lear's elephantine nose, like Cyrano's, was the centerpiece of his unhappiness. Its great length seems to have descended to him from his mother; the bulbous outline was a gift from his father. Anyone born with a nose like that is bound to hide himself in obscurity, or else, braving the wounds or the pity the world inflicts, do something extraordinary to compensate for it. Cyrano fought the Moors; Lear wrote numerous limericks about nose victims and, in a happier frame of mind, about nose philosophers or even nose conquerors.

There was an Old Man, on whose nose,
Most birds of the air could repose;
But they all flew away, at the closing of day,
Which relieved that Old Man and his nose.

There is a young lady, whose nose,
Continually prospers and grows;
When it grew out of sight, she exclaimed in a fright,
"Oh! Farewell to the end of my nose!"

There was an old man of Dunrose;
A parrot seized hold of his nose.
When he grew melancholy, they said, "His name's Polly,"
Which soothed that old man of Dunrose.

There was an old man in a barge,
Whose nose was exceedingly large;
But in fishing by night, It supported a light,
Which helped that old man in a barge.

There was a Young Lady whose nose,
Was so long that it reached to her toes;
So she hired an Old Lady, whose conduct was steady,
To carry that wonderful nose.

There was an Old Person of Tring,
Who embellished his nose with a ring;
He gazed at the moon, every evening in June,
That ecstatic Old Person of Tring.

There was an Old Man with a nose,
Who said, "If you choose to suppose,
That my nose is too long, you are certainly wrong!"
That remarkable Man with a nose.

There was an old man of West Dumpet,
Who possessed a large nose like a trumpet;
When he blew it aloud, it astonished the crowd,
And was heard through the whole of West Dumpet.

There was an old person of Cassel,
Whose nose finished off in a tassel;
But they call'd out, "Oh well!—don't it look like a bell!"
Which perplexed that old person of Cassel.

One poem in particular seems to sum up Lear's nose sufferings. It reads rather like compressed Tennyson and Edgar Allan Poe in their most mystical moods. From the point of view of lyrical quality it can be highly praised, because if the reader can contrive to forget the ludicrous subject matter, he might find himself heavy with grief, marvelously moved by the bottomless desolation of the creature called a Dong, drearily searching for an unattainable love. Nor need we doubt that the true identity of the creature is Mr. Nonsense himself; he is even drawn wearing a false nose.

THE DONG WITH A LUMINOUS NOSE

When awful darkness and silence reign
Over the great Gromboolian plain,
  Through the long, long wintry nights;—
When the angry breakers roar
As they beat on the rocky shore;—
  When Storm-clouds brood on the towering heights
Of the Hills of the Chankly Bore:—

Then, through the vast and gloomy dark,
There moves what seems a fiery spark,
   A lonely spark with silvery rays
   Piercing the coal black night,—
   A Meteor strange and bright:—
Hither and thither the vision strays,
   A single lurid light.

Slowly it wanders,—pauses,—creeps,—
Anon it sparkles,—flashes and leaps;
And ever as onward it gleaming goes
A light on the Bong-tree stems it throws.
And those who watch at that midnight hour
From Hall or Terrace, or lofty Tower,
Cry, as the wild light passes along,—
   "The Dong!—the Dong!
"The wandering Dong through the forest goes!
   "The Dong! the Dong!
"The Dong with a luminous Nose!"

Certainly noses had a dread meaning in Lear's psychic life. There is remarkable and distinct evidence of it in the fact that his caricatures of himself are distinguished by a small, dainty nose. As he grew older and fatter, the pleasing knob he drew grew even more modest until, in the end, Lear, as seen by Lear, became a sort of sophisticated Mr. Pickwick.

But he never really possessed that cheery little button. It was only wishful thinking.

X
Marriage
Fantasies

Among Lear's lifelong attachments was his affection for the poet Alfred Tennyson and his wife Emily. With Emily, indeed, he enjoyed a closer sympathy than with almost any other living person, and she was his faithful correspondent during the long, lonely years abroad.

When Lear first met Tennyson, the poet was forty and had just been named poet laureate of England. Lear, however, had esteemed him long before that, because he had a notion that he did his best artistic work when in the soulful mood inspired by Tennyson's lyrical descriptions of moldering castles and mystic moonlit groves. Tennyson's admiring friends were willing to tramp with him for hours over the moors while he spouted for them his latest lengthy work, and Lear was pleased to join their company.

At the Tennyson household Lear became a popular after-dinner entertainer. Seating himself at the piano, he would sing the master's words in heartfelt tones, accompanying them by melodies that poured from his own talented fingers. Several of Lear's musical settings for Tennyson's poems became very well known and were much appreciated. Four of them were published in 1853.

Professional musicians often found fault with Lear's songs, but possibly some envy was mingled with their criticism. Tennyson himself preferred Lear's settings to more professional efforts, because, he said, they did not smother the words, but "threw a diaphanous veil" over them. A certain archbishop, after hearing Lear deliver himself of "Home They Brought Her Warrior," was so moved that he exclaimed, "Sir, you ought to have half the laureateship!"

Lear's own favorite, and Tennyson's, was "Tears, Idle Tears," but once when he was playing it for a young lady, singing "with not much voice, but an expression of gravity and pathos on his face," he suddenly substituted "Hey Diddle-diddle, the Cat and the Fiddle" to the same air.

More than anyone else, gentle Emily Tennyson recognized that beneath Lear's expansiveness and humor, his charm and generous love of his friends, lay an immense craving for affection. She detected the cavernous lack in his emotional makeup, the lack of a child rejected by his mother, and with exquisite sensitivity, tried to heal and comfort him. "I have a deep, sad feeling," she wrote to him once, "we must help each other and love each other, those who at all understand each other."

Lear wrote of Emily:

I should think, computing moderately, that 15 angels, several hundreds of ordinary women, many philosophers, a heap of truly wise and kind mothers, 3 or 4 minor prophets, and a lot of doctors and schoolmistresses might all be boiled down and yet their combined essence fall short of what Emily Tennyson really is.

Lear was an uncle to Emily's sons as they grew up— "very darling chaps indeed," he thought them—and through the years his relationship with her became ever more deep and significant. Unfortunately the friendship with Alfred loosened and some coolness developed between the two men. It is quite possible that Alfred, who very much liked to be the center of the stage, did not enjoy sharing Emily's attention with a large, plump, whiskery quasi-son, about whose health and well-being his frail wife constantly felt uneasy. In addition, Lord Tennyson's enormous success as a poet, which kept all England hanging on his every limpid word for decades, had somewhat gone to his head.

Great poets in those times, being popular entertainers, received the same type of adulation that we offer today to "superstars." In his later years Tennyson became generally autocratic and demanding, hurtful and inconsiderate toward his family as well as his friends. On one occasion he had promised to buy two of Lear's drawings of Corsica; then he abruptly changed his mind. Lear, probably with financial need aggravating his hurt feelings, lost his temper. Both of them exploded in a rage, and Lear stomped upstairs to pack his things and leave the poet's house.

Emily smoothed the row over, but it was never really mended, and Lear wrote in a tone of rare unkindness about the atmosphere in the poet laureate's home: ". . . a contradictory mixture of high-souled and philosophical writings, combined with slovenliness, selfishness and morbid folly."

This animosity did not prevent him from cherishing all his life a particular ambition: to illustrate Tennyson's poems. He felt strongly there was poetry in the depths of his being, but overpowered by the giant talent and reputation of his friend, he did not suppose that it could emerge in words. Instead, he thought he had it in him to match the antique romance of Tennyson's literary landscapes with graphic poems, the finest fruit of his travels in classic lands. "Very few painting coves," he wrote to Hallam Tennsyon, the poet's son, with typical modesty-vanity, "—however superior to this child as artists—could illustrate the landscape allusions in your Father's poems with such variety and perhaps accuracy."

Once a lady had said of Lear that his father had been a poet and his mother a photographer. In his work on the Tennyson illustrations, he seemed to wish to prove this symbolic statement. The project kept him busy on and off for years. He would disappear for months into a landscape paradise such as Switzerland and return with scores of sketches, which he would then finish at his leisure and in the proper mood. There were to be about two hundred selected scenes in the end. Reproduced and published as a set, they would represent the culmination of his life's work as an artist. One can easily understand that in an age that considered Tennyson's poems to be the apex of literary beauty, such a project was exciting and grandiose. Furthermore, Tennyson approved of the scheme and encouraged it.

Over the years Lear actually did complete the two hundred scenes, but there was trouble afoot. No satisfactory method of reproduction could be found, "by which I can eventually multiply my 200 designs by photographs or autographs or sneezigraphs or any other graphs." He was thinking of using lithography, but when some lithographs were made, they did not satisfy him. In one way or another, the grand project kept petering and fizzling out.

Like all of Lear's ambitions, this plot to stroll into immortal realms on the coattails of Alfred Lord Tennyson failed to take his own proper worth into consideration. How could he know that the creations of his own mind would remain triumphantly afloat through the wildest storms of time, while the poet laureate's rhythmic philosophies, for all their lovely imagery, would in another age seem overly simple, or warmed up, or even meaningless?

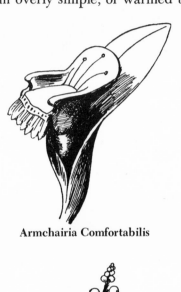

Armchairia Comfortabilis

Bassia Palealensis

Bubblia Blowpipia

Crabbia Horrida

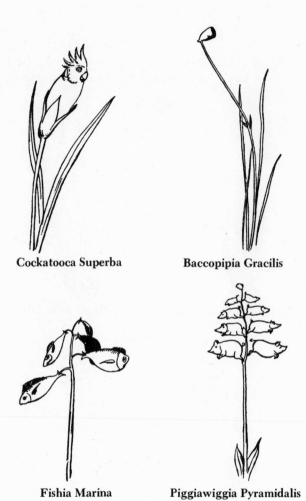

Cockatooca Superba   Baccopipia Gracilis

Fishia Marina   Piggiawiggia Pyramidalis

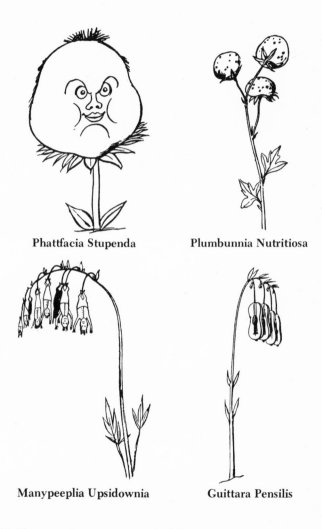

Phattfacia Stupenda   Plumbunnia Nutritiosa

Manypeeplia Upsidownia   Guittara Pensilis

In his Nonsense Botany, Lear poked fun at the high-sounding Latin
and Greek names.

XI

Tears, Idle Tears

When Lear was a young man, his very intense emotional nature had been preoccupied and perhaps satisfied by close friendships with bachelor companions. But as the years passed, one by one they slipped away from him into another kind of life, which lay on the other side of the marriage ceremony. It was not that he lost them exactly; he never lost a friend on this account, because their wives easily became addicted to him. However, bachelors can sit up half the night talking and planning trips and mountain climbs; they can drink too much and snooze with their socks on and wake up for breakfast at noon. No such disorderly conduct can survive a wife.

Lear loved domesticity, and he loved to be included in his friends' intimate family circles and to be the favorite uncle of their children. In his rootless life, spent knocking about the English colonies of the Mediterranean, shuttling between the Continent and home, and everywhere holding "his eggsibishuns" where English families abroad could come knocking at his door, he must have met more than his share of marriageable daughters. Still, he never married.

Aside from his illness, which, of course, was a major deterrent, Lear, from childhood on had had an ingrained conviction that he was far too ugly for any woman to want to marry. "No doubt," wrote one who knew him, "he was ugly." His nose was "elephantine" and, being shortsighted, he was obliged to wear a pair of eyeglasses perched on it like a silly moth. He was baldish and moved with an awkward, slouchy locomotion that was not made more romantic by a steadily increasing potbelly. So convinced was he of his terrible appearance that with sublime pride he aggravated it by dressing carelessly, his clothes hanging about him like a tent, far too big, and in no sense shaped to his figure. Dress, he believed, was of no concern to an ugly man—and he was beyond redemption.

As if sickness and repulsive appearance were not enough to exclude him from the marriage bazaar, there was the ever-present, soul-shriveling problem of money. His work as a landscape painter was far from financially successful. He had intermittent strokes of really good fortune when one of his "important" or more impressive works won a prize, or was bought by some prestigious earl to decorate a country seat, or was purchased by an institution at an agreeable price. But these bonanzas were not frequent. For the most part, Lear continued to sell to the tourist trade for middling prices or even low ones, and all his life he was never more than a few hundred pounds ahead of his debts.

No settled income, no home, endless anxiety, no prospects—how could he ask a woman to share these miseries with him? Of course, there was a perfect solution—he might marry a girl with some money of her own.

Emily Tennyson, with a woman's instinct to act as matchmaker, determined to settle Lear's future for him satisfactorily. She had a well-to-do young lady marked out, a Miss Cotton, who, upon hearing Lear in a soulful voice rendering Tennyson's poems into song, had declared herself deeply moved. Lear retreated from Emily's suggestions in silence. In an effort to get him jumping out of the bush, she started the false rumor that Miss Cotton was about to be married to a vicar, but to her sorrow Lear contemplated the news that the lady was about to slip through his fingers with complete indifference.

There were, however, other romantic attachments that caused him more agitation. In 1855, after he had spent the years following the political turbulence in Italy wandering homelessly around the Mediterranean, Lear came to rest in Corfu, where his taciturn friend Frank Lushington had been appointed a judge of the Supreme Court governing the British protectorate in the Ionian Islands. Lear was enchanted with the islands, describing their coastal scenery enthusiastically as "pomskizillious and gromphibberous," but Lushington's serious-minded devotion to his duties and his silent, exclusive nature left Lear suffering agonies of loneliness. He found himself much taken up with the Cortazzi family, an Italian gentleman, his English wife, and their two daughters, particularly Helena.

"I believe I have found myself wishing sometimes that I was 20 years younger," he wrote to Emily, "and had, I won't say 'more,' but 'any' money."

It is to be expected that the women Lear especially admired were uncommon women, and Helena was. She had not only translated Tennyson's poems into Italian, but had also set them to music. In fact, she and Edward Lear had much in common, and he wrote to Holman Hunt that he was at least "half in love."

"There are two awful sisters here (I call the house Castle Dangerous)," he wrote. "English . . . so simple and good, and so full of poetry and good taste and grace; and all the nettings whereby men are netted—I begin to feel I must either run for it or rush to extremes."

In the end he ran for it. He remained a friend of the Cortazzi family, but the weak flame that had flickered up for Helena swiftly sputtered out.

A far more serious contender for the title of the unfortunate Mrs. Lear was Augusta Bethell, whom Lear called "Gussie." She was the daughter of Richard Bethell, one of Lear's oldest friends, who later became Lord Westbury, the Lord Chancellor. It was for the entertainment of this gentleman's grandchildren (Gussie's nieces and nephews) that Lear wrote his *Story of the Four Little Children Who Went Around the World*.

Lear had watched Gussie grow up. In 1862, when he was fifty, she was a young woman of twenty-four, whose company brought him a happiness and tranquillity that he had seldom known. Wonder of wonders, she seemed to like his company equally well; moreover, she was gentle and humorous and shared all his interests in life—in time, she was even to become an author of children's books.

Lear loved Gussie dearly and described her in his diary as "dear little Gussie, who is absolutely good and sweet and delightful." Then he added the ominous comment, "BOTHER!"

While enjoying every minute of Gussie's presence, Lear never gave her an inkling of his feelings, but for years he toyed with the thought of marrying her. He returned for a summer to England and stayed at her home, seriously wanting to broach the subject to her, but still overcome with pity for her sad lot should she consent to do so. "Poor Gussie!—but how to decide? If her life is sad, united to mine would it be less so? or rather—would it not be more so?"

He was in a quandary, and let months and then years go by without popping the question.

The year 1866 found him in Corfu again and wondering, "Would Gussie like to live here?" He became so nervous and depressed over his doubts that he developed neuralgia and various skin complaints. He resolved never to return to England rather than subject Gussie to the possible risk of being asked, and of consenting, to marry him.

Lear's doubts and indecisions about Gussie gave rise to a remarkable poem, entitled "The Courtship of the Yonghy-Bonghy-Bò," which is surely one of the most amazing products of the English language, because, while it is shocking nonsense from beginning to end, it squeezes the heart with a painful sadness and leaves it haunted not only by the sadness of unrequited love but by a loneliness far vaster—pure loneliness, in fact.

I

On the Coast of Coromandel
Where the early pumpkins blow,
In the middle of the woods
   Lived the Yonghy-Bonghy-Bò,
Two old chairs, and half a candle,—
One old jug without a handle,—
     These were all his worldly goods:
     In the middle of the woods,
     These were all the worldly goods,
   Of the Yonghy-Bonghy-Bò,
   Of the Yonghy-Bonghy-Bò.

II.

Once, among the Bong-trees walking
Where the early pumpkins blow,
To a little heap of stones
Came the Yonghy-Bonghy-Bò,
There he heard a Lady talking,
To some milk-white Hens of Dorking,—
"'Tis the Lady Jingly Jones!
"On that little heap of stones
"Sits the Lady Jingly Jones!"
Said the Yonghy-Bonghy-Bò,
Said the Yonghy-Bonghy-Bò.

III.

"Lady Jingly! Lady Jingly!
"Sitting where the pumpkins blow,
"Will you come and be my wife?"
Said the Yonghy-Bonghy-Bò.
"I am tired of living singly,—
"On this coast so wild and shingly,—
"I'm a-weary of my life;
"If you'll come and be my wife,
"Quite serene would be my life!"—
Said the Yonghy-Bonghy-Bò,
Said the Yonghy-Bonghy-Bò.

IV.

"On this Coast of Coromandel,
"Shrimps and watercresses grow,
"Prawns are plentiful and cheap,"
Said the Yonghy-Bonghy-Bò.
"You shall have my chairs and candle,
"And my jug without a handle!—

"Gaze upon the rolling deep
("Fish is plentiful and cheap)
"As the sea, my love is deep!"
Said the Yonghy-Bonghy-Bò,
Said the Yonghy-Bonghy-Bò.

This poem is certainly Lear's long-bottled-up proposal to Gussie, though one to which she could never reply. It is almost certain that Gussie returned his sentiments and tried to encourage him, as far as a Victorian lady decently could. One winter when he had settled in Nice, she took the trouble to travel there with her sister, "to my delight," wrote Lear, "who with them walked and drove about thro' all the livelong day."

By 1867 matters were at a boiling point. "I do not say I am decided to take this leap in the dark, but I say that I am nearer to doing so than I ever was before."

Lear now made a fatal mistake. In this delicate matter, which might have brought together two of the most sensitive hearts that ever beat as one, he asked the advice of outsiders. His friend Fortescue had married a Lady Waldegrave, a woman of great wealth and sophistication, who was one of Lear's most generous patrons, and she, judging from the standards of her world, advised him that since Gussie had no money, it would be unkind for Lear to ask her to share his financially troubled existence.

Not yet discouraged, Lear then consulted Gussie's sister Emma. We cannot know what was in this young woman's head—possibly she genuinely disliked the thought of Gussie's marrying a man almost thirty years older and in terrible health. In any case, she definitely discouraged the match and crushed his hopes by telling him that such a marriage was utterly impossible.

All was now over. "Accept a lonely destiny ... and make the best of it," he wrote in his diary.

And so Lear never married, and Gussie married someone else. On her wedding day she inherited twenty thousand pounds. Her husband was in wretched health, much worse off than Lear, completely paralyzed, a hopeless invalid.

V.

Lady Jingly answered sadly,
And her tears began to flow,—
"Your proposal comes too late,
"Mr. Yonghy-Bonghy-Bò!
"I would be your wife most gladly!"
(Here she twirled her fingers madly)
"But in England I've a mate!
"Yes! you've asked me far too late,
"For in England I've a mate,
"Mr. Yonghy-Bonghy-Bò!
"Mr. Yonghy-Bonghy-Bò!

It was the last time he was to contemplate having a family of his own. Lear wrote bitterly to Lady Tennyson: "Nobody ought to marry at all, and ... no more people ought ever to be born ... the world to be left to triumphant chimpanzees, gorillas, cockroaches and crocodiles."

THE YONGHY BONGHY BÒ.

On the coast of Co - ro - man-del,   Where the

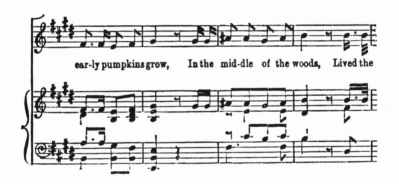

ear-ly pumpkins grow,   In the mid-dle of the woods,   Lived the

Yonghy-Bonghy- Bò ;   Two old chairs and half a candle,   One old

THE YONGHY BONGHY BÒ

jug without a han-dle; These were all his worldly goods, In the

mid-dle of the woods, These were all the world-ly goods, Of the

Yong - hy Bong - hy Bò, Of the Yong - hy Bong - hy Bò.

XII
Villa
Emily

Lear spent the winter of 1870 in lodgings in Cannes, on
the French Riviera. It was there that he wrote the most
famous of his nonsense songs, "The Owl and the Pussy-
cat," a poem whose enduring popularity proves that the
comic enchantment of "psychedelic art" is by no means a
modern discovery.

1

The Owl & the Pussy-cat went to sea
In a beautiful peagreen boat
They took some Honey, & plenty of money,
Wrapped up in a Fivepound note.

2

And the Owl looked up to the moon above,
And sang to a small guitar,
"O lovely Pussy! O Pussy my love!
What a beautiful Pussy you are!"

The poem was written for a little girl who was sick in bed. She was the daughter of the historian and essayist John Addington Symonds, a chance neighbor of Lear in Cannes, in whose house he quickly began to feel at home.

Lear was at that time getting hard to please in the matter of places to spend the winter, and was longing for a place to settle down. It is true that from time to time on his travels there were pleasing incidents. Once an old lady in a hotel told him how, years ago, she had heard a poem of Tennyson's set to the most beautiful music. Lear went to the piano, and in a voice "hollow with age, but with great style," sang it and brought tears to the old lady's eyes. "Why," she exclaimed, "that is exactly the setting I referred to: do please tell me whose it is."

"It is mine," replied Lear, and continued to sing several

more songs to her, while other hotel guests clustered
around the door.

On another occasion, while he ate in a hotel dining
room, he observed a plump little woman peering curiously
through the door at him. Presently a tall man with a
gleaming great beard approached him and said, "My wife
wants to know if you are Mr. Lear, and [to say] that she
would be pleased to renew her acquaintance with you."

The tall man turned out to be Crown Prince Frederick
of Prussia, father of Kaiser Wilhelm II (the German
monarch of the First World War). His wife was Vicky, the
princess royal, Queen Victoria's daughter. Neither she nor
her brother, the future Edward VII, had ever forgotten
the jovial young man who used to be their mother's
drawing master.

Now, however, moments like this were insufficient.
Lear was touching sixty, and he was growing weary of his
wandering life. Not that he could no longer enjoy a tour or
be captured by a lovely sight, but as he grew older, melancholy began to take precedence over his normal
ebullience. Besides, he was a man whose life's energies
were being squandered on tasks for which he was not really cut out, and his continuing lack of success with his
painting could only plunder him of strength and courage.
Nevertheless, humor, enthusiasm, a marvelous sense of the
grotesque and the comic did not abandon him altogether.
In 1871 the *Nonsense Songs* were published. If their com-
edy is threaded through with a deep pessimism of the soul,
it is a quality that endows Lear's nonsense with a beauty
beyond the ordinary.

Since his days on Corfu, Lear had been attended by a
manservant, Giorgio, who in the course of their years

together had become less servant than friend. "Giorgio," said Lear of him, "though he very seldom speaks, speaks sense when he speaks at all." Mr. Sense cared for Mr. Nonsense with complete devotion, and Lear treasured him, but Giorgio, too, was getting old. He, after all, had the worst of the hard work that their wandering life entailed, and Lear finally decided that they both deserved to come to rest in a settled home.

For some time he ranged up and down the Mediterranean coast, looking for a site, and his choice finally fell on San Remo on the Italian Riviera. There he bought a piece of land and began to build a house, which he mysteriously named the "Villa Emily." The Emily so honored may have been Lady Tennyson, but there is an equal chance that she was a great-niece of Lear whom he had never seen, but to whom he intended to leave the house upon his death.

Lear was never a man to keep accounts, and the expenses of construction soon ran much higher than he had expected. In his embarrassment, he turned for help to Lord Derby. This Lord Derby was not, of course, the old gentleman who had first rescued him from the steward's room at Knowsley years ago, nor yet his son, the thirteenth earl, Lear's first patron and the collector of the Knowsley zoo; it was the fourteenth earl, who had by this time come into the title. Once he had been "a little boy in black velvet," one of the youngsters Lear had entertained in the nursery with the first nonsense limericks.

Lord Derby responded to Lear's cry for help in the most amiable manner, with a fat commission for a painting. Lear, sentimentally touched, wrote, "So I began my San Remo life with the same Knowsley patronage as I began life with at eighteen years of age."

By a strange coincidence, during the entire period of the building of the Villa Emily, commissions came in from all directions, from one and another of Lear's friends. Nothing in his writings at the time shows that he suspected that a plot was afoot. It is only when we look back at this sudden passion for Lear landscapes among people who already owned more than enough of them that we wonder if it was not prompted by a kindly hint from Lord Derby.

Villa Emily was a roomy, comfortable Mediterranean villa, its square design not unlike that of Lear's childhood home at Holloway. There was a "painting-room" for Lear —the first he had ever had in his life—a gallery where he could exhibit his paintings to possible buyers, and plenty of extra rooms for visiting friends. A large and luxuriant garden surrounded the house, which Lear, not in the least suspecting how domesticated he really was, had intended at first to leave to the care of a bandy-legged gardener. Soon, however, he found himself absorbed in the fascination of picking off caterpillars and coaxing things to grow and flower. In this paradise, amid the sound of "twittery birds," peace began to assuage his melancholy, and after Foss, the tomcat who had "no end of a tail," had joined the household and become his inseparable companion, happiness was as complete as it could be.

Lear worked placidly on his plentiful commissions, and in his spare time resumed his cherished series of illustrations for Tennyson's works. He felt at last that he belonged to something, if only to a house, a garden, Giorgio, and Foss. He did not suspect for a minute that he really belonged to everybody, even when *More Nonsense* was a huge Christmas success in 1871. He wrote to Chichester Fortescue, marveling how queer it was "that I am the man as is making some three or four thousand people laugh in England all at one time."

But his pleasure at this frivolous success was nothing compared to his excitement not long after, when Fortescue was honored by the queen with a peerage, as Lord Carlingford:

> O! Chichester, my Carlingford!
> O! Parkinson, my Sam!
> O! SPQ, my Fortesque!
> How awful glad I am!

No sooner had Lear begun to feel blessedly at rest at Villa Emily than a disturbing invitation arrived. His friend Thomas Baring, who had become Lord Northbrook, had been appointed viceroy of India, and he wanted to take Lear to India with him "free of expense for a year of sightseeing."

This exotic colony had made Queen Victoria into an empress and had evoked the curiosity of all Englishmen, but in spite of the generosity of Northbrook's offer and the possible profit to himself—for people then were as eager to see paintings of India as we are to see motion pictures of the moon—Lear was far from anxious to exchange his cozy new nest for the pomp and protocol of a viceregal court. Lear always cheerfully admitted that he had quite a large dose of what was then called "Bohemian" blood, at least as much as any artist or creative person needed, and he wrote, "Always accustomed from boyhood to go my ways uncontrolled, I cannot help fearing I should run rusty and sulky by reason of retinue and routine."

For a while Lear tried to talk himself out of the journey, using rather an un-Bohemian argument: Would it not

seem giddy of him to take off for India just when he had
settled down in a new home? More seriously, there was
his health to consider. He had recently added heart
trouble to his list of afflictions, and the physician had for-
bidden him to run upstairs fast, let alone face the un-
known hardships of a Far Eastern land. He hesitated so
long that he missed traveling with the viceroy's party, but
Lord Northbrook pressed the invitation nevertheless,
urging Lear to follow at his expense.

Lear finally set out for India, but he happily managed to
miss the last ship at Suez and was forced to return to San
Remo. There he was able to spend a whole year, not only
preparing himself mentally to tackle the Indian journey a
second time, but picking up a few commissions for paintings of Indian scenes. Evidence of his blooming
orientalism and curiosity about the East is the poem he
wrote that winter, which became a favorite:

> *Who or why, or which, or what,*
> *Is the Akond of Swat?*
> *Is he tall or short, or dark or fair?*
> *Does he sit on a stool or a sofa or chair,*
> *or* SQUAT,
> *The Akond of Swat?*
>
> . . . . .
>
> *Can he write a letter concisely clear*
> *Without a speck or a smudge or smear*
> *or* BLOT,
> *The Akond of Swat?*
>
> *Do his people like him extremely well?*
> *Or do they, whenever they can, rebel,*
> *or* PLOT,
> *At the Akond of Swat?*
>
> . . . . .

At night if he suddenly screams or wakes,
Do they bring him only a few small cakes,
          or a LOT,
     For the Akond of Swat?

Does he beat his wife with a gold-topped pipe,
When she lets the gooseberries grow too ripe,
          or ROT,
     The Akond of Swat?

It was as well that Lear did stay close to home that winter, for he had the pleasure of learning that his nonsense books had come to the attention of the House of Commons, where a member said that Parliament every year published a much more celebrated *Book of Nonsense* called the *Statute Book*. Lear wrote in his diary: "Fancy being really in a speech. . . . Sich is phame."

In the autumn of 1873, he and Giorgio made their second assault upon India. It took them twenty-seven days from Genoa to Bombay where, immediately upon landing, Lear was seized with his old excitement upon seeing a new country. This one was a novel feast of treats to the eye. "Violent and amazing delight," he wrote, "at the wonderful varieties of life and dress. . . . O fruits! O flowers! O queer vegetables!"

But he had not the sheer physical stamina to support his curiosity. He began to complain about the incessant traveling by train, carriage, cart, boat, elephant, and horseback, and the nights spent in noisy hotels, dak bungalows, tents, and railway carriages, eating strange and indigestible food. Nor did life in the viceregal palace in Delhi charm him. He found his rooms "preposterously magnificent, not to say awful . . . too many servants, too many

distractions, too much necessity of being polite to bores
. . . hatefuly fussy life: no rest in Hustlefussabad."

In Lucknow, his luggage somehow got lost on the day
he was scheduled to ornament the viceroy's procession of
state by riding on an elephant, "without proper clothes,
chilled and miserable. Can't tell what to do in all this miserable hullabaloo and luggagelessness."

Taken together, his Indian letters and journals form a
long litany of crotchets and discontents, but most of them
were the result of poor health. He had sudden moments of
enthusiasm for the vast wonders of the mysterious subcon-
tinent—the improbable flowers, the flaming colors, and the
"most beautiful of all earthly buildings," the Taj Mahal—
for an elephant smoking a hookah, or water pipe, and for
two hundred thousand Hindus "flumping" in the Ganges
under the sunrise—"squash!"

He loved Benares, the holy city, and described it as
"startlingly radiant," and he made some excellent and
impressive paintings of the sweep of the ghats, or stairs,
above the River Ganges. In fact, during this trip he
dispatched to England 560 drawings, plus nine small
sketchbooks. Despite illness, Lear was quite accurate
when at this time of his life he described himself as "a very
energetic and frisky old cove."

As always, he was at his most cheerful when in some
out-of-the-way hotel he could gather a group of children
around him and produce his parade of mad birds and
animals. One little girl, watching him draw an owl,
enchanted him by saying, "Oh, please, draw a pussycat
too!" She carefully explained that these creatures had
gone to sea in a pea-green boat and that her entire class
had had to learn by heart a poem to that effect.

In July of 1874, the *Bombay Times* published Lear's im-

pressions of India in a poem entitled "The Cummerbund," which captured as well as can be the menacing
loveliness of a tropical jungle:

> *She sate upon her Dobie,*
> *To watch the Evening Star,*
> *And all the Punkahs as they passed*
> *Cried, "My! how fair you are!"*
> *Around her bower, with quivering leaves,*
> *The tall Kamsamahs grew,*
> *And Kitmutgars in wild festoons*
> *Hung down from Tchokis blue.*
>
> *Below her home the river rolled*
> *With soft meloobious sound,*
> *Where golden-finned Chuprassies swam,*
> *In myriads circling round.*
> *Above, on tallest trees remote,*
> *Green Ayahs perched alone,*
> *And all night long the Mussak moaned*
> *Its melancholy tone.*
>
> *And where the purple Nullahs threw*
> *Their branches far and wide,—*
> *And Silvery Goreewallahs flew*
> *In silence, side by side,—*
> *The little Bheesties' twittering cry*
> *Rose on the fragrant air,*
> *And oft the angry Jampan howled*
> *Deep in his hateful lair.*

All of these strange Hindi words were really the com-
monplace terms of any Anglo-Indian household. A *dobie*
is a laundryman, a *punkah* a fan, a *nullah* a dry water
course. The tall *kamsamahs* and *kitmutgars* are only

butlers and waiters, and a *tchoki* is a policeman. A *chuprassie* is a messenger, an *ayah* a children's nurse, and a *goreewallah* a groom. A *bheestie* is a water carrier, and he carries his water in a *mussak* made of skin. A *jampan* is a carrying chair.

The villain of the poem, the dread *Cummerbund*, who eventually gobbles up the fair lady, is, as everyone knows by this time, nothing but an Indian gentleman's waist sash. It is only Lear's odd ear for evocative sound that brought these harmless words together in a mad marriage of the comic and the sinister.

Lear spent fourteen months in India. Then Giorgio fell seriously ill, and Lear tended him until he recovered. By that time he, too, was ill with a strained back, and it was clear that the Indian journey was getting to be too much for the two elderly men. So, although it troubled Lear to have missed seeing more of India, they went home in January of 1875.

Lear and Giorgio returned to the Villa Emily to find that in their absence it had been broken into by burglars. The rooms were in a shambles, cupboards had been ransacked and their contents scattered about. Little, if anything, had been stolen—there was nothing much to steal in the house of a "dirty landscape painter"—but Lear was very upset at the thought that his beloved house had been penetrated by brutal and thoughtless strangers. Later, though, he found that the incident provided him with an excellent excuse whenever anything was wanted and could not be found; the loss could always be blamed on the burglars.

So he settled down to completing his Indian commissions and to resuming his pet project, the illustrations for the works of Tennyson.

XIII
Paradise
Lost

As sometimes happens to people when they are getting old, Lear and Giorgio had to face, within a short span of time, the news of a sudden avalanche of illness and death. One of Lushington's small daughters, Lear's godchild, died; his last remaining sister went blind. Emily Tennyson remained in very frail health, and in Corfu, Giorgio's wife, mother, and brothers died, one after the other.

Giorgio himself was ill, and there seemed to be no hope for his recovery. Lear had never properly recovered his own strength after the Indian journey, but since his servant had expressed a wish to die in Corfu, he set out to accompany him there.

The journey, undertaken in winter, was beset by blizzards and storms at sea, and it proved to be too much for Lear. He was obliged to turn back, heavyhearted, leaving Giorgio in the care of his son. As it turned out, however, the following year Giorgio made a remarkable recovery, and he was able to return to San Remo and resume his duties at the Villa Emily, assisted by two of his sons.

Visits from the Lushington family and their children and from other friends cheered Lear and improved him. There was "a plethora of friendship, all in a lump," he wrote. His spirits rose to such an extent that he said, "I should be rather surprised if I am happier in paradise than I am now."

During this pleasant interlude Lear produced *The Pobble Who Had No Toes*, which was written for one of Lushington's daughters. The Pobble proves his creator's recovered spirits by coming through a variety of horrendous adventures not much the worse for wear, thanks to Aunt Jobiska's comfortable philosophy:

> *It is a fact the whole world knows*
> *That Pobbles are happier without their toes.*

Then one day calamity tumbled about Lear's ears. Some years earlier, when he had acquired the land for the Villa Emily, his money had not stretched far enough to enable him to buy the strip between his garden and the sea. He had asked the owner to inform him if he intended selling the strip, and had trusted that he would do so.

Now, in the autumn of 1875, an ominous chop-chop of axes sounded amid the music of the twittery birds— workmen were chopping down the olive trees. Inquiries revealed that the land had been sold, and that a huge hotel was to be built upon it, "nothing less than a diametrical damnable blazing 5-story hotel," cutting off his view from the sea, the sun from his garden, and the light from his studio.

Two English people and a "Gerwoman" were at the

bottom of it, and upon these three Lear vented his wrath in letters that flew right and left to all his friends. For a time his new peace of mind was totally destroyed, and his happiness in the Villa Emily fled away.

He hated to think of leaving the house and garden he had learned to love, yet from the first sound of "chop-chop" he could think of little else. There was no question that he must find somewhere else to live. He had the choice of selling the Villa Emily at a financial loss—for of course the value of his property would be much reduced by the presence of the monstrous hotel—and build anew nearby; or else of leaving San Remo—Europe, in fact—altogether. In his anger, he saw himself emigrating to New Zealand, where his niece Emily lived.

In the end Lear decided to remain in San Remo, selling at a loss and building anew a house that had "only the road and the railway between it and the sea, so unless the Fishes begin to build, or Noah's Ark comes to anchor below the site, the new villa . . . cannot be spoiled." The new villa was to be an exact replica of the old one; otherwise, Lear explained, "Foss would not like it."

Foss's specifications were therefore faithfully adhered to, and the new house was baptized "Villa Tennyson," which seems to dispose of any doubt as to which Emily was closer to Lear's heart. Again his troop of helpful earls rose wonderfully to the occasion with financial assistance. It is well that they did, and that he did not have to depend upon his latest *Nonsense Book*. Its increasing popularity had led him to hope that for the first time in his life he would receive a just reward for his labor, but unfortunately the publication was in the hands of a publisher who chose that very year to go bankrupt. Lear never recovered the money that was owed to him in royalties from his successful work.

Lear's last visit to England was in the summer of 1880. He was pleased and flattered to find that he had become something of a society lion. The plentiful invitations to dinner parties and other social events were not, this time, so much a tribute to his talents as a conversationalist and after-dinner entertainer as to his achievements as an author and indeed as a landscape painter, for some of his finer works had found distinguished buyers.

He was elated one day, upon visiting a stately home of England, to be confronted with a large painting of his own, "let into the wall in a vast black frame, all the room being gilt leather! Never saw anything so fine of my own doing before." After that, he said, he walked about for the rest of the day, smiling benignly upon every soul he saw.

Still, the happiest hours were those spent at the hearthsides of his friends, and when he visited them to say goodbye, he knew he would never see many of them again.

The following year the new villa was completed, and Lear went to work with restored enthusiasm to re-create the pleasant garden he had left behind.

> *And if you voz to see my roziz*
> *As is a boon to all men's noziz*
> *You'd fall upon your back and scream—*
> *O Lawk! O crickey! it's a dream!*

XIV
I Think
I'll Go to Bed

In the years that followed his last visit to England, Lear's health failed him. Gradually he became feeble, crippled by rheumatism, blind in the right eye, and hard of hearing. He tottered around his new house.

> *He only said, "I'm very weary,*
> *The rheumatiz," he said,*
> *He said, "It's awful dull and dreary,*
> *I think I'll go to bed."*

Yet so extraordinary were Lear's vitality and his habits of work, that sometimes, when the pain released him, he rose at dawn in enormous spurts of energy and painted all day until the brush fell from his hands.

As he grew old, his thoughts turned more and more to religion. As a boy, living with his sister Ann, he had usually accompanied her to church, and for a while in adulthood he had continued this convention. Then he realized that it was habit and duty that took him to church rather than interest in the services; indeed, in time he came to be repelled by the outer aspects of religious faith. His thoughts sought out the essential spirit of Christianity, which he felt laid only one duty on a man—to love his "fellow-bean." He could not even hear with pleasure the intoning of the Creed, for it seemed to him sheer nonsense that only Christians could accept salvation and that "the Almighty damns the greater part of His creatures."

Years before, on one of his first long travels in the Mediterranean, Lear had visited Mount Athos, a place famous in Greek legend, and also in the earliest Christian legends because it was said to have been visited and first consecrated by the Virgin Mary herself. Certainly this community of monks is very old, one of the oldest continuous foundations in Christendom, and in Lear's time it was pervaded by an atmosphere of extreme piety, deliberately cultivated for the edification of tourists. Lear had no patience with this. "I do not say hypocrisy—but I say falsehood . . . and ignorance," he wrote with abrupt irritation to Ann, ". . . the name of Christ on every garment and at every tongue's end, but his maxims trodden underfoot. . . . God's world and will turned upside down, maimed and caricatured . . ."

An honest Turk with six wives, a Jew working hard to feed his children, he thought, had more in common with Christ than "these muttering, miserable, mutton-hating, man-avoiding, misogynic, morose and merriment-marring, monotoning, many-mule-making, mocking mournful, minced-fish and marmalade-masticating Monx."

Lear's dislike of public worship and display of religion

increased as he grew older—no matter if the dean of West-minster was one of his lifelong friends. At the same time, though, his sense of genuine, personal religion deepened. Once, on reading a religious publication, he marked the following passage: "Though I know neither the time nor the manner of the death I am to die, I am not at all solicitous about it, because I am sure that He knows them both, and that He will not fail to comfort and support me under them."

He believed in life after death. "The longer I live, the more I think I perceive . . . our present existence is merely a trifle in comparison with what may be beyond, and that there *is* a life beyond this it seems to be the greatest of ab-surdities to deny or even to doubt of."

Yet when Lear came to conceive of what sort of place the world beyond might be, he proved to be just as much a fussy customer as he was on the earthly plane:

> When I go to heaven, if indeed I go—and am surrounded by thousands of polite angels—I shall say courteously, "Please leave me alone:—you are doubtless all delightful, but I do not wish to become acquainted with you;—let me have a park and a beautiful view of sea and hill, mountain and river, valley and plain, with no end of tropical foliage:—a few well-behaved cherubs to cook and keep the place clean—and —after I am quite established—say for a million or two years —an angel of a wife. Above all, let there be no hens! No, not one! I give up eggs and roast chicken forever."

It is possible that on Lear's extensive travels through untrodden mountain villages, he had been offered far too many hen roosts to sleep in.

By the eighth decade of his life, Lear had become a very

well-known personality, one of the sights of the Continent for traveling Englishmen. After moving into the Villa Tennyson, he threw open his gallery every Wednesday to throngs of them. It is more likely that they came to stare at Lear rather than at his pictures, though, because they usually went away without buying, and Lear again and again sadly noted in his dairy, "No sail, no sail."

As his health worsened, he closed his gallery except by special appointment. Sometimes when the bell rang, he went himself to answer it, and if he thought the visitor looked unappealing or unpromising, he put on a long face and in a weak voice explained that he never showed his paintings nowadays, being much too ill for it. But for welcome guests he could still glitter and glow with jollity.

The queen would have liked to visit Lear on one of her trips to the south of France, but the protocol involved in her crossing the Italian border daunted her—to Lear's relief. "I dislike contact with royalties," he wrote, "being a dirty landscape painter, apt only to speak his thought [s], not to conceal them." Yet he was extremely pleased when Crown Princess Frederick of Prussia took the trouble to visit his home; she was "the most absolute duck of a Princess imaginable."

His friends came to see him, and when they were not with him, they were busy arranging for the sale of paintings so that serious financial worries should not plague his old age. Lord Derby wrote, assuring him that there were at Knowsley still some walls that did not bear a work by Lear.

The visit that restored his liveliness and zest for a while —and at the same time an old agitation—was that of. Gussie Bethell, the only woman in his life to provoke his serious love interest. After all those years, she still had the power to awaken longings and regrets. "I wish I were not so dam old," he remarked—for Gussie was a widow now and presumably fancy free. She came with two nieces and stayed at nearby hotel, spending most of her days with Lear. Again he became taken up with the old dilemma, whether or not to ask Gussie to marry him. It was consideration for her, once more, that forbade him to broach the topic. Still, Gussie was extremely fond of him, and she might well have been glad, if only he had spoken, to be his companion and loving nurse for the rest of his life.

When she left, Lear noted in his diary, "I miss her horribly."

Of Lear's unofficialy family the first to die was Giorgio, who had been with him for twenty-seven years. Lear had a tablet raised to his memory at San Remo, beside the spot he had chosen for his own grave.

Then, in 1884 he wrote his last nonsense poem, which concerned his "aged Uncle Arly, sitting on a heap of barley." This gentleman had two significant possessions, a first-class railway ticket in his hatband and a cricket on his nose—an enviable person, one would have thought, except that his shoes were far too tight. It is all nonsense, of course—but a fitting summary to Lear's life.

In 1886, John Ruskin, England's greatest critic, the man whose personal tastes had substantially shaped the cultural life of mid-Victorian England, wrote in the *Pall Mall Gazette* a few stunning words: "I don't know of any author to whom I am half so grateful for my idle self as Edward Lear. I shall put him first of my hundred authors."

His praise came too late to enrich Lear, but it was not too late for him to feel crowned with glory.

He was working mostly now at finishing the ill-starred

Tennyson illustrations, doubly doomed because his eyesight was failing and he was half blind.

Then Hallam Tennyson, the poet's son, wrote to him saying that an American publisher was bringing out an edition of his father's poems and would like to see Lear's drawings. The publisher arrived at Lear's home in May of 1887 and found him sitting up for the first time in weeks. He was shown the two hundred drawings, which he thought "very interesting and would add greatly to the interest of our proposed edition." He did not fail to notice Lear's eagerness. Evidently the reproduction and publication of these drawings on which he had worked for half a lifetime were "the dearest wish of this old gentleman's heart. I fear the sensation of pleasure is a rare thing to him in his sad old age."

Nevertheless, this final phase of the Tennyson scheme came to grief. Only after Lear's death was a small book published, limited to one hundred copies, signed by Tennyson, and containing three poems and twenty-two of Lear's landscape illustrations, reduced to a very small size. If Lear had seen them, he would surely have shed tears over the death of his dream.

But by now the end of his days was coming nearer, and he wrote to Gussie asking her to visit him again. Again she came, and Lear once more perplexed himself with the momentous question. "Once or twice the crisis nearly came off," he wrote in his diary, ". . . yet nothing occurred beyond her very decidedly showing me how much she cared for me." Poor Gussie!

The last time Lear saw his beloved was when he paid her a farewell visit at her hotel. As he left, he was weeping.

Then in the autumn of 1887, Foss, the tailless tomcat, his daily companion for seventeen years, died, and was buried in the garden. Now Lear was quite alone.

He sat on the rose-hung terrace of the garden he had planted and loved. His tame pigeons fluttered about him and he lived in a kind of pastoral peace, soothing to his melancholy.

Crippled by rheumatism, spending much of his time motionless, he wrote, "My life seems to be more and more unsatisfactory and melancholy and dark . . . on the whole I don't know if I am living or dead at times."

He grew weaker, his memory began to fail. One day toward the end of January, he said to his servant, "My good Giuseppe, I feel that I am dying. You will render me a sacred service in telling my friends and relations that my last thought was for them. . . . I cannot find words sufficient to thank my good friends for the good they have always done me."

Not long after that, in the early morning hours of January 29, 1888, he died.

In his own mind he had failed at many things. As a painter, he had not been fully appreciated—even today his work is treasured only because of historic fame as the author of the nonsense books. He never married, never had children of his own, although he understood and loved children as perhaps few people ever do.

Yet he did have something—the greatness of one who had loved his "fellow-beans."

Edward Lear's Published Works

TRAVEL BOOKS

Views in Rome and Its Environs. 1841.
Illustrated Excursions in Italy. 1846.
Illustrated Excursions in Italy. Second Series. 1846.
Journal of a Landscape Painter in Greece and Albania. 1851.
Journal of a Landscape Painter in Southern Calabria. 1852.
Views in the Seven Ionian Islands. 1863.
Journal of a Landscape Painter in Corsica. 1870.

NONSENSE BOOKS

The Book of Nonsense. 1846.
Nonsense Songs, Stories, Botany and Alphabets. 1871.
More Nonsense. 1872 (published Christmas, 1871).
Laughable Lyrics. 1877.
Queery Leary Nonsense. 1911.
Lear Coloured Bird Book for Children. 1912.

OTHER PUBLICATIONS

Illustrations for the Family of the Psittacidae. 1832.
Gleanings from the Menagerie at Knowsley Hall. 1846.
Tortoises, Terrapins and Turtles. 1872.
Tennyson, *Poems.* Illustrated by Edward Lear. 1889.

Letters of Edward Lear. Edited by Lady Strachey. 1907.
Later Letters of Edward Lear. Edited by Lady Strachey. 1911.

Bibliography

Bleuler, Eugene, *Textbook of Psychiatry*. New York, The Macmillan Company, 1944.

Davidson, Angus, *Edward Lear*. Harmondsworth, Middlesex, Penguin Books, 1950.

Kretschmer, Ernst, *The Psychology of Men of Genius*. New York, Harcourt, Brace & Co., 1931.

Noakes Vivian, *Edward Lear*. Boston, Houghton Mifflin, 1969.

Nonsense Omnibus. London and New York, Frederick Warne & Co., 1943.

Pfeiffer, John, *The Human Brain*. New York, Harper & Brothers, 1955.

Sheldon, W. H., *Varities of Delinquent Youth*. New York, Harper & Brothers, 1949.

Index

123

N

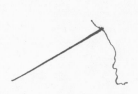

n

N was once a little Needle,
 Needly
 Tweedly
 Threedly
 Needly
 Wisky—wheedly
 Little Needle !

O

o

O was once a little Owl,
 Owly
 Prowly
 Howly
 Owly
 Browny Fowly
 Little Owl !

P

p

P was once a little Pump,
 Pumpy
 Slumpy
 Flumpy
 Pumpy
 Dumpy, Thumpy
 Little Pump !

T

t

T was once a little Thrush,
 Thrushy
 Hushy
 Bushy
 Thrushy
 Flitty—Flushy
 Little Thrush !

U

u

U was once a little Urn,
 Urny
 Burny
 Turny
 Urny
 Bubbly—burny
 Little Urn.

V

v

V was once a little Vine.
 Viny
 Winy
 Twiny
 Viny
 Twisty-twiny
 Little Vine !

Z